A Delightful Tapestry of Homespun Magic

Creating beautiful and artistic handcrafts is in itself a magical act. Now, you can use your craft projects to further imbue your home with a magical atmosphere and evoke magical energy.

Magical Needlework explores the versatility of this magical art and offers a myriad of hands-on projects, ideas and patterns submitted by a wide spectrum of people within the spiritual community. You will discover magical powers contained within various symbols, numbers, shapes, textures, stitches, and weaves.

Sew a fairie dress for Midsummer Night's Eve and dance in the moonlight…safeguard your home with an herbal protection charm…crochet a pentacle wallhanging…knit a meditation mat for balance in your life…quilt an herbal soap bag and infuse it with magical success…and much more.

Like a fine quilt, Morrison has gathered the magical fibers of needlecraft and stitched them together with humor, warmth and insight; an invaluable resource.

— *Patricia Telesco*
author of A Victorian Grimoire
and A Kitchen Witch's Cookbook

About the Author

Dorothy Morrison was trained in the arts of the needle at an early age. She lives the magical life in the boot heel of Missouri with her husband and teenage son. They share their home with two feisty Labrador Retrievers, Sadie Mae and Jonah, various tropical fish, and a large assortment of African violets. She is a Wiccan High Priestess of the Georgian Tradition, and founded the Coven of the Crystal Garden in 1986. An avid practitioner of the ancient arts for more than twenty years, she teaches the Craft to students throughout the United States and in Australia and is a member of the Pagan Poet's Society.

Also an archer and bowhunter, Dorothy regularly competes in outdoor tournaments and holds titles in several states. Her other interests include magical herbalism and stonework, Tarot work, and computer networking with those of like mind.

To Write to the Author

If you would like to contact the author or would like more information about this book, please write to her in care of Llewellyn Worldwide. We cannot guarantee every letter will be answered, but all will be forwarded. Please write to:

Dorothy Morrison
℅ Llewellyn Worldwide
P.O. Box 64383, Dept. K470-7
St. Paul, MN 55164-0383 U.S.A.

Please enclose a self-addressed, stamped envelope for reply or $1.00 to cover costs. If outside the U.S.A., please enclose an international postal reply coupon.

Magical Needlework

35 ORIGINAL PROJECTS & PATTERNS

Dorothy Morrison

1998
Llewellyn Publications
St. Paul, Minnesota 55164-0383
U.S.A.

FIRST EDITION

First Printing, 1998

Cover design: Anne Marie Garrison

Cover photo: Doug Deutscher

Chapter opening illustrations: Kathleen Kruger

Interior photos: Tom Grewe

Additional interior art: Llewellyn Publications

Editing and book design: Amy Rost

Patterns on pages 92, 94–95, 100, 103, 105, 107, 129–130, 137, 151, 184–187, 189–190, and 192 electronically rendered by Hannah Shirley. Pattern on page 191 electronically rendered by Becca Allen.

Cover projects rendered by Becca Allen.

Interior projects rendered by Cynthia Ahlquist, Becca Allen, Georgette Bruhn, Jody Cunningham, Dreamspinner, Cindy Hatcher, Julie Hanavan-Olsen, Marcia Herbster, Kitty Laust-Gamarra, Susan Lund, Dorothy Morrison, Mary Lou Rost, Astrid Sandell, InaRae Ussack, and Lily Winter.

Wearable projects modeled by Cindy Hatcher.

The following people contributed project designs to this book; their work is used with their permission. Contributors: Aaydan (Fort Hood, Tex.); Alodi (Field-n-Forest); Susan M. Baxter (Crafts for the Craft from Starwood); Dreamspinner (Willowbrook, Ill.); Elayne (Wichita, Kan.); Karen Everson (Moongate Designs); Julie Hanavan-Olsen (Urtha Lun Creations); Mayrose (Carbondale, Ill.); Miss Chiff (Misc. by Miss Chiff); Myth H (Myth H Designs); InaRae Ussack (*Crafts/Craft Magazine*).

The untitled poem at the beginning of Chapter Seven was used with the permission of Elizabeth J. Campbell.

Projects Featured on Front Cover

Lacy Leaf Edging
A Witch's "Blessed Be" Sampler
Goddess Bag
Harmony-in-Your-Life Patchwork Heart
Celtic Knotwork Bookmark
Enchanted Notebook or
    Book of Shadows Cover
Knitted Bookmark
All-Purpose Poppet
Stone/Crystal Cups

Refer to the List of Projects, page x, to find these projects throughout the book.

Library of Congress Cataloging In-Publication Data

Morrison, Dorothy, 1955–
    Magical needlework: 35 original projects & patterns / Dorothy Morrison.
        p. cm.
    Includes bibliographical references.
    ISBN 1-56718-470-7 (pbk.)
    1. Needlework—Patterns.   I. Title.
TT753.M67 1998
746.4—dc21   97-52214
                                                        CIP

Publisher's Note

Llewellyn Worldwide does not participate in, endorse, or have any authority or responsibility concerning private business transactions between our authors and the public. All mail addressed to the author is forwarded but the publisher cannot, unless specifically instructed by the author, give out an address or phone number. The publisher has not tested the techniques included in this book, and takes no position on their effectiveness.

Llewellyn Publications
A Division of Llewellyn Worldwide
P.O. Box 64383, Dept. K470-7
St. Paul, Minnesota 55164-0383

Printed in the U.S.A.

Forthcoming Books from Dorothy Morrison

Everyday Magic
(1998, Llewellyn Publications)

The Whimsical Tarot
(1998–1999, deck and book; U.S. Games Systems, Inc.)

In Praise of the Crone
(1999, Llewellyn Publications)

Dedication

Trish, Vivie, Myth H, Miss Chiff and Elayne,
And my wonderful students (who didn't complain),
Susan, Barb, Lydia and dear InaRae,
Mayrose and Aaydan, sweet Rosie and Gay,
Auralii of the loom and spinning finesse,
Spook (who ignored the continual mess!),
Mark, for the original name of this book,
Julie, who helped me and knew what it took,
The Lord, the Lady, the Muses—the Ancient Ones, too...
With hugs, love and kisses—this book is for you!

Contents

Chapter One

Spellwork and Needlecraft: A Basic Primer 1

Proper Timing for a Spell Crafts the Magic Very Well • Setting the Mood: Creating a Magical Atmosphere • Weaving the Spell With Color, Medium, and Symbol • Preparation and Consecration the Working Implements • Cleansing the Materials

Chapter Two

Magical Sewing: Assembling the Magic 11

Letting Fabric Choose You • How Does Your Energy Flow? Considering Fabric Design and Texture • Scissors, Pins, Needles, and Notions Set the Magic into Motion • To Go High-Tech or Knot • What's Sew Magical? Giving Mundane Articles a Magical Flavor

Chapter Three

Magical Patchwork and Quilting: 39
Piecing Together the Magic

Geometrical Patchwork • Free-Form Patchwork (Crazy Quilting) • Curved Patchwork and Appliqué • Magically Symbolic Patchwork Designs • Numbers and Blocks and Magic! Oh My! • Setting the Magic in Motion with Templates, Pencils, and Scissors

Quilting: Layering the Magic • Stitched Quilting Designs That Mirror Intent and Purpose • Stitching the Layers Binds the Magic

Chapter Four   **Magical Embroidery: Interlacing the Magic** 83

Stitches in Time: Weaving the Rhyme • Counted Cross Stitches in a Row Make the Magic Really Grow • Magical Results Received Depend Upon the Proper Weave • How Many Strands Can Be Threaded Through the Eye of a Needle? • Enchanting Knots and Stitches

Chapter Five   **Magical Crochet: Chaining the Magic** 111

The Magical Basics of Crochet • Stitch Abbreviations • Magical Crochet Stitches • Magical Granny Squares: An Exercise in Versatility • Threads and Yarns: Natural Fiber Versus Man-Made Fiber

Chapter Six   **Magical Knitting: Connecting the Magic** 139

The Magical Basics of Knitting and Purling • Stitch Abbreviations • Magical Knitting Stitches and Patterns • Casting On Begins the Spell

Projects

Chapter Two

Magical Sewing:
Assembling the Magic

Chapter Three

Magical Patchwork and Quilting:
Piecing Together the Magic

Chapter Four

Magical Embroidery:
Interlacing the Magic

Chapter Five

Magical Crochet:
Chaining the Magic

Chapter Six

Magical Knitting:
Connecting the Magic

Preface

Magic is a change in condition or situation by ritual means. There is nothing more magical than needlecraft. It has all the properties of a spell: intent, concentration, repetition, and changes in condition or form. Although needlework is inherently ritualistic, a project intended for enchantment has more intensity and magical power than a project undertaken casually.

Magical needlecraft works equally well for solitary practitioners and large groups. Any spellwork can be tailored to fit this medium. A spell can be performed anywhere—in your home, on the road in the car, in the doctor's office waiting room, even while visiting relatives. No one has to know that a magical ritual is in progress.

I grew up in a family that held dear the genteel customs of the Deep South, including needlecraft. I spent hours with a tapestry needle or crochet hook, struck with awe at how the skills of my foremothers lived through me. I wondered if they had experienced the same delight in color blending, stitch arrangement, and composition. Through my stitches, I felt the influence of my predecessors, was aware of their tastes, and knew that their hands guided mine as I worked.

The full impact of magical needlecraft hit me when I was trying to write a safe travel ritual for our cross-country move. Annoyed because the words wouldn't come, I turned to embroidering on a scrap of Aida cloth. The Ancients flipped a switch, and the cosmic lights came on; I saw the ritual in following a pattern and repeating stitches. I fashioned the scrap into an amulet bag, filled it with the appropriate herbs and stones, and blessed it. We completed our journey in perfect safety.

Today, many practitioners consider needlecraft a viable magical vehicle. They praise it for ease in handling, the ability to travel smoothly over the bumpiest cosmic roads, and the dependable performance found only in more complicated magical systems. I urge you to give magical needlecraft a spin, too. It's fun, it's easy, and it works for everyone!

Acknowledgements

Whether on the magical plane or the mundane, nothing comes into being without a culmination of efforts. This book is no exception. Many people gave generously to make this project a reality. They researched enthusiastically, shared their personal experiences with magical needlecraft and gave me a gentle prod when I needed it. Heartfelt thanks to all of them, but especially to the folks listed here.

To my husband, Spook, who ate snacks instead of supper, did without me on hunting trips, and served me coffee in bed on Saturday mornings.

To Trish, Barb, and InaRae, who patiently listened, commiserated, advised, encouraged, and held my hand from start to finish.

To Gay, Merry, and Gypsy, who crocheted swatches, delivered hugs, and forced me to look at each crisis with new perspective.

To Jan Kingsford, who took care of my business correspondence, and knitted swatches until her fingers were sore.

To Myth H, who believed in this project, spent countless hours researching and copying, and saw enough of the Federal Express courier to be on a first name basis.

To Auralii, who took the time to make that wonderful spinning and weaving video, patiently answered all my questions, and was there every time I needed her.

To Julie, who infused me with her enthusiastic zest for the spiritual path, and to J. D., Dan, Hannah, Emma, and Cheyenne for sharing this remarkable woman with me.

To Mayrose, who edited and corrected my grammar, shared ideas, and nudged me in the right direction.

To Elayne, Nina, Miss Chiff, Valeka, Heidi, Procion, and the many PodNet users who shared their magical needlecraft experiences with me.

To Kausalaya, who brought Chandra into my life so she could be shared with the world.

To Janis Cortese, who graciously shared her Wiccan/Quilting comparison list for use in this project and to Dragonfly, who allowed the use her binding charms.

To Becca Allen, Cindy Hatcher, Kitty Laust-Gamarra, Jody Cunningham, Marcia Herbster, Susan Lund, Cynthia Ahlquist, Astrid Sandell, Georgette Bruhn, Lily Winter, and Mary Lou Rost, who graciously took time from their busy schedules to stitch the projects pictured in this book, and who kept my thoughts of a nervous break-down at bay. Special thanks to Cindy Hatcher for modeling the magical wearables.

But most of all, to the reader. By reading this book, you continue to keep the magic of needlecraft alive and vibrant—just as it was meant to be from the beginning of humankind.

Goddess bless you—all of you—and may your needles never snap!

Spellwork and Needlecraft

A Basic Primer

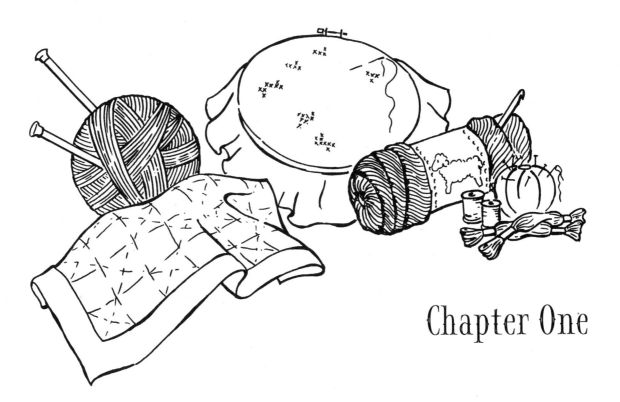

Chapter One

A note I wrote to Santa Claus when I was six years old read like this:

Dear Santa,
Please bring me a new bicycle for
Christmas. Don't bother with the training
wheels, though, 'cause they're for babies
and kids who aren't as smart as me....

Well, Santa took me at my word. The bicycle and Christmas Eve arrived around the same time, but the training wheels never made the trip.

The bike was huge and blue, and I thought it was the most fabulous contraption ever invented—until I took the first ride down that bumpy gravel road. "Ride" isn't a very good word for what happened, because after that trip Mama had to wrap me in so much gauze and tape that I looked like a mummy.

My problem was that I didn't understand anything about bicycling basics and didn't know how much there was to learn. Incorporating spellwork into needlecraft is much like learning to ride a bicycle, for both crafts involve attitude, environment, timing, mechanics, and path choice. You have an edge—training wheels in the form of this primer. It contains suggestions, ideas, and information about the fundamentals of magic. Use it to your advantage and enjoy your journey through the magical world of needlecraft—it is a trip you will never forget.

Proper Timing for a Spell Crafts the Magic Very Well

Timing is an important part of all spellcasting, and weaving a spell with magical needlecraft is no exception. Many magical practitioners work spells in conjunction with the phases of the Moon, because they control the waters of life such as the tides, the menstrual flow, and the physical body, which consists largely of fluid. The Moon is also linked to emotional responses, and pure, properly channeled emotion energizes magic. The practitioner usually realizes greater success when working during a phase of the moon that is in harmony with the magical intent.

The Moon waxes when She grows in the sky from invisible to full, and efforts that require growth can be accomplished during this part of the cycle. This period is good for fresh starts, new love, and beginnings, and it benefits those wishing to build businesses, friendships, partnerships, and financial prosperity. The energy of the waxing Moon is additionally suitable for the planting of herbs, the development of psychism, and an increase in health and well-being. "Growth" and "enhancement" are the key words for this phase.

When the Moon begins to shrink from full to dark, She is on the wane. The waning Moon is a good time for magical efforts requiring peaceful elimination. Use this phase to end an undesirable eating pattern, break a bad habit, or remove yourself from a stressful partnership or situation. Its energies favor any magical working that requires calm separation or recession. The key words for the waning Moon energy are *shrinkage* and *removal.*

When the Moon is full, Her energy is at its peak. Any magical effort benefits greatly from the potency of this period. When working with difficult projects or spells, the practitioner can use the energy of the full Moon to boost magical intent. *Amplification* and *intensity* are key words for the vibration of the full Moon.

Some magical individuals use the dark time of the Moon as a period of rest. They find it useful for regeneration, relaxation, and gathering power for the creative phase of the waxing Moon.

Others prefer to take advantage of dark Moon energies. Some practitioners use this time to meditate, enhance psychic power, or delve into past life memories so they can better understand current difficulties. Dark Moon energy lends itself to divination where the truth of the matter is an issue. Key words for the influence of the dark Moon are *regeneration* and *uncovering*.

A situation may be so pressing that waiting for the proper phase is not an option. What then? By changing your magical perspective and using a bit of cosmic psychology, you can still achieve the desired goal. For example, if your finances are a complete disaster and the Moon is waning, you might request a decrease in poverty.

If your instincts tell you to wait for a particular Moon phase, use the time to plan your project. That way, you will be ready to start when the proper phase arrives.

Setting the Mood: Creating the Magical Atmosphere

The right frame of mind is the most important factor in making a magical needlecraft project successful. You can coax your attitude into cooperating by creating an environment suitable for magic. There are as many ways to do this as there are threads in a tapestry.

Some people invoke a magical frame of mind by surrounding themselves with items that hold personal magic for them. If this idea appeals to you, try setting up a personal altar in your magical work area. The altar doesn't have to look magical; it can look more like a decorative arrangement if that is more to your liking. For example, a practitioner I know has a small altar in her bedroom. It holds a straw plate, a cup of black beans, stones, a bowl of dried rose buds, and two votive candles. A special cookie jar and a basket of Pagan-oriented greeting cards sent by friends and relatives rest there, too. Because each item is magically symbolic to the practitioner, her whole frame of mind changes every time she enters the room—and that creates the perfect attitude for successful magic.

Others burn candles. Yellow candles are an excellent choice for magical needlework efforts, as yellow vibrates toward the creative energy flow. Candles in shades of purple work well, too, especially if you feel a need for spiritual guidance in performing the current spellwork. If neither of these colors appeal to you, try white. It is a culmination of all colors of light and vibrates toward every energy in the spectrum.

Another approach is to visualize an appropriately colored sphere around you and the project. It is perfectly all right to cast the

Circle beyond the walls of the room. See a Circle of colored light growing around you, its walls rising high above and far below, enveloping you in a large, transparent, empowered sphere of color. When you stop working for the day, dissolve the sphere by mentally erasing it. Beginning at its top and bottom, simultaneously dissolve both sectors until only the original circle remains, then visualize its disappearance, as well.

I find it helpful to place a basket of herbs and stones on my work table as a reminder of my magical intent and creativity. If you prefer to create a magical atmosphere by incorporating stones and herbs, you don't have to accumulate a large supply of either. More than likely, you already have a tin of cloves in your kitchen cabinet, and clove is the herb used most successfully in inspiring a magically creative atmosphere. The stones that vibrate toward these qualities are also fairly common. Chrysoprase, a pale green stone known for its joyous properties, simply exudes inspirational energy. Citrine, golden topaz, and orange calcite are also terrific circulators of creative energy. These work well either in combination or alone, because the energy of each stone is independent and does not require blending with the others.

Some people like to scent the air or their bodies to set the mood. Incenses, oils, and potpourris may be obtained from your local occult shop or by mail order from those businesses listed in the Resource Section. Since blends can be known by different names, be specific about the scent or ingredients you are looking for. If you can't find a scent to your liking, phone your favorite shop and ask them to formulate a more suitable blend. Most shops offer this service and will be happy to accommodate you, or try one of the all-purpose recipes given here.

Inspiration Incense

(This formula works best when prepared during the waxing to full Moon.)

Ingredients

> pine needles or
> pine bark shavings
>
> cloves
>
> crushed daylily or
> white lily petals
>
> hyacinth petals

The amount of each ingredient will vary depending on which of the following recipes you use.

Incense

To prepare as an incense, use a mortar and pestle, a coffee mill, or a blender to grind a handful of pine needles or bark shavings with 1 teaspoon of cloves. Add 2 teaspoons each of crushed dried lily and hyacinth petals and mix well. (Three drops of each essential oil may be substituted for the flower petals.) Sprinkle a bit at a time on burning charcoal.

Anointing Oil

One vial each of the following essential oils:

> Pine
>
> Clove
>
> Lily
>
> Hyacinth

1. Combine 3 drops of each essential oil into 1 ounce of vegetable oil, swirl to mix, and use;

or

2. Combine 2 teaspoons of each ingredient with ½ cup of vegetable oil, and slowly warm in a slow cooker for 8 to 10 hours. When the fragrance suits you, strain the oil from the herbs and allow the mixture to cool. Bottle and use.

Stove-Top Potpourri

Stove-top potpourri is quick and easy to prepare. Place equal portions of the herbs or essential oils into a small non-metal saucepan filled with water and let it simmer on the stove. The scent permeates the house, a constant reminder that magic is in the air.

Creativity Incense

(This formula works best when prepared during the waxing to full Moon.)

Ingredients

> hyssop
>
> verbena
>
> clove
>
> galangal
>
> coffee (ground, not prepared or instant)

Again, the amount of each ingredient will vary depending on which of the following recipes you use.

Incense

For incense, mix equal parts of the ingredients and burn on a block of charcoal, or use 3 drops essential oil of each herb with a pinch of ground coffee.

Oil and Potpourri

Prepare anointing oil and stove-top potpourri as described in the Inspiration formula.

Music can help to set the mood. Birdsongs might lift your spirit as you work. Or perhaps to you, blessed silence is the sweetest music of all. Sitting down to your project with a cup of herbal tea or your favorite beverage, if done habitually, signals the inner self that your special time is at hand. Some people like to wear a special item of clothing, a hat, or a piece of jewelry to help invoke their magical creativity.

Magical needlecraft is a unique form of enchantment and constructing a magical working environment is a personal adventure. The method you use to set the mood is immaterial, but creating a magical atmosphere that relates to the project and to your personality is invaluable.

Muses/Magical Space Ritual

This ritual is one of the best ways I have found to create an appropriate atmosphere for magical needlecraft. It entices the creative spirit of the Muses to flow through you and aids in claiming specific space for magical work.

Materials

- yellow candle
- incense (Creativity, Inspiration, or a scent that you enjoy)
- small dish of water
- small dish of salt
- picture frame with glass insert (whatever size you like)
- felt or fabric piece cut to the inner frame dimensions
- needlecraft symbols (see ideas in the following section)
- white glue

Gather symbols of the needle arts that you enjoy. For example, if you like to embroider, gather several skeins of floss in colors that appeal to you. If laces, ribbons, and buttons are more to your liking, collect an assortment of those. Crochet artists might want to use doilies for this ritual, while knitters might find a collection of yarn scraps and gauge swatches more appropriate. If magical patchwork suits your tastes better, amass a small assortment of brightly colored fabric remnants. Use whatever says "magical needlecraft" to you.

Sit comfortably and take several deep breaths to ground and center. Inhale through your nose, pulling the energy of Mother Earth well into your body. Then exhale fully from your mouth, releasing any unwanted energy back into the Earth. Do this until you feel totally relaxed.

Pass the symbols through the incense smoke, then holding them in your hands, blow on them three times, saying:

I give you air to breathe.

Taking care not to burn yourself or the symbols, pass them over or through the candle flame, touch them to the spot between your eyes, and touch them to your heart. Say:

I give you light, vision, and passion.

Sprinkle them lightly with water and say:

I give you the waters of life to drink.

Sprinkle them with salt and say:

I give you roots that you might sprout, grow, and bud.

Call the Muses to aid you in all magical needlecraft endeavors by saying:

**Muses, live and breathe and grow
Grant your visions—let them flow
Through my mind and through my hands
Like endless grains of finest sand.**

Remove the backing from the frame, cover it with the piece of fabric or felt, and secure the edges with glue. Arrange the symbols collage-style on the fabric-covered piece. Let go of your ordinary mindset and yield totally to the Muses. Feel Their creative energies surge through your center and out through your hands. Let Them guide you in design and form. Secure the completed arrangement with glue.

Insert the collage into the frame and secure it well. Consecrate the picture and the workspace to the Muses, saying:

**Muses, come and work through me
Guide my hands, my mind, and free
Inhibitions in this space
Magic flows with speed and grace.**

Thank the Muses for Their help and hang the picture in a prominent place on your work area wall. Each time you enter the room to work, spend a few minutes meditating on the collage. This will help you connect with the Muses and put you in the right frame of mind for magical work.

Weaving the Spell With Color, Medium, and Symbol

Color

The next step in working a magical needlework project is to consider an appropriate color scheme for the spell. Let's pretend that you wish to construct a magical quilt for the baby of a dear friend. Before going with the pastels that are "normal" for crib quilts, decide whether pale colors suit your purpose. Exactly what qualities do you wish to give to this fresh, new life? (For help with color scheme and combinations, see the section on magical colors in Appendix B.)

Some time ago, I made a magical crib quilt for a new baby. My magical intention was to bestow the gifts of wisdom, spiritual growth, vitality, strength, and good health upon the child. I chose several shades of teal green and combined them with the same number of shades of reddish purples, then put them together with unbleached muslin.

Purple is the color of wisdom and spirituality, red belongs to vitality and strength, blue vibrates toward health, and green relates to growth. The pale cream color of the unbleached muslin symbolically "lit the child's path." Though I only used three shades, I managed to get all the "quality vibrations" I wanted by choosing combination colors.

Medium

After deciding upon the project's purpose and colors, explore appropriate media. Should the project be crocheted, sewn, embroidered, pieced and quilted, beaded, or a combination of the above? Also work through the practical considerations; it wouldn't be safe to make a delicately beaded magical toy for a young child. Your own preferences are also a major consideration. If you despise knitting but love to embroider, toss the knitting yarn aside and grab the embroidery floss. After all, you are the magician, and the components, construction, medium, and ingredients of the spell are entirely up to you.

Symbol

Finally, consider the symbology you wish to use in the project. For instance, if you were constructing a beaded amulet bag to hold a love charm, a single heart might be used, or perhaps the ankh (which is the symbol of the planet Venus).

Shapes aren't the only way to incorporate symbology. Numbers could be used as well. In the case of the amulet bag, you might wish to work the beads in multiples of six, as six is the number of love and harmony.

I usually make an outline first, as it provides a handy list of supplies and magical vibrations and serves to keep my mind on the intent during the creation process. Creating the outline is also a minor ritual in keeping with the project, and the more time you spend on magical ritual of any type, the more powerful the magic becomes.

Preparation and Consecration of the Working Implements

Because tools for magical ritual hold power, they are usually consecrated before their initial use. The same is true of the implements used in magical needlecraft—scissors, pins, needles, hooks, spindles, shuttles, and such. It is a good idea to keep these items together in a special box (I prefer one divided into several compartments), because it keeps things organized and close at hand.

Preparing implements for spellwork is a simple process. Only a few basic rules apply, and they can be easily adapted to your situation and personality. Begin the consecration by sorting the needlework tools into the box and organizing them. When the arrangement pleases you, a "blanket" consecration and blessing may be used. Holding the box aloft, say something like:

> Oh Brigit, Goddess of Needlecraft,
>   these tools I offer you.
> I consecrate them in your name and
>   ask your blessing to
> Make them ease my workload and
>   magically magnify
> My intentions for each project and all
>   that does imply.
> Please lend to them your wisdom and
>   give to them your skill.
> I charge these instruments in your name.
>   So be it, as I will!

Generally, Brigit, the Goddess of arts, crafts, and needlework is an excellent choice for invocation; however, if other deities are more suitable to you (Clotho the Spinner, Athena, Spider Woman, Isis, Ixchel, Hestia, and Vesta come to mind here), invoke them instead.

Some magical needlecrafters prefer to bless their supplies each time they begin a new project. This is extremely helpful when adding new implements, notions, or materials to your regular accumulation and is also beneficial in reinforcing the magic in existing tools. The following invocation works beautifully for blessing or strengthening existing magic:

> I call out to My Lady,
> Goddess of the Moon,
> To bless these gifts
> From the weaver's loom,
> The threads and needles
> And all supplies
> Bless [name the tools]
> And be my guide!
> I, [your name], ask this
> Of free mind and free will,
> These blessed gifts of guidance,
> Insight and sacred skills!
> So Mote It Be!

> — *From Miss Chiff of Misc. by Miss Chiff*

Cleansing the Materials

Before beginning any magical project, it is a good idea to purify the materials with the Elements to cleanse them of all negativity. Yarns, crochet threads, ribbons, or fabrics for which dry cleaning is recommended can undergo this symbolic purification.

Gather Inspiration or Creativity incense; frankincense; a small white candle (a birthday cake candle will do); a small bowl of water, and a small amount of salt. Light the candle and the incense, then take a few deep breaths to ground and center.

Pass the material or fiber through the incense smoke three times and invoke the Element of Air, saying:

> Come to me now, oh winds of the East.
> Whirl and twirl 'til the magic has ceased.
> Blow through this fiber and energy raise.
> Bring inspiration and blow away haze.
> Blow out negative energies! Positivity send!
> To purify this fiber, Your power please lend!

Being careful not to burn the fiber or yourself, pass the material over the candle flame three times and invoke the Element of Fire, saying:

> Come to me now, oh Southerly fires.
> Warm light, pure strength—
>   add flame to desires.
> Cast out all energies previously mundane.
> Add life to this fiber with pure light
>   and flame.
> Burn out negative energies! Positivity send!
> To purify this fiber, Your power please lend!

Invoke the Element of Water by carefully sprinkling the fiber three times and saying:

> Come now, oh waters of the Western port.
> Tides rise and fall, and all harm abort.
> Rinse away energies of harm and of pain.
> Wash over this fiber with your
>   gentle spring rain.
> Wash out negative energies! Positivity send!
> To purify this fiber, Your power please lend!

Finally, sprinkle the fiber with three pinches of salt (one pinch at a time) and invoke the Element of Earth, saying:

> Come, earthly power to me from the North.
> Give your strength and stability—
>   give your support.
> As your soil is fertile, this fiber shall be.
> Nourish this fiber, as you nourish the tree.
> Cast out negative energies! Positivity send!
> To purify this fiber, Your power please lend!

Leave the fiber or material in the spot where you cleansed it until the candle and incense extinguish themselves. Though hand-washing might be in order when cleansing delicate fabrics, the washing machine works well for sturdy washable fibers, such as cotton or linen. Add the recommended amount of detergent, a handful of table salt, and wait for the load to agitate. (If you don't have plastic pipes, forgo the salt, because it is corrosive to metal. Instead, place three beans or peas in a sock, knot the top and toss it in.) Then invoke the spirits of Water and Earth, saying:

> Oh pure, clear water with soap and suds,
> Cleanse this fabric of all ill-will,
> Liken it to spring's sprouting buds—
> A pure blank canvas, my spell to fill.
> Oh purest water with soap and salt
>   (beans/peas)
> And fiber grounded to the Earth,
> Good vibrations, please exalt (increase)—
> Add fertileness to this spell's girth.

Watch the water flow through the fabric for a few moments and visualize all negativity washing away, leaving nothing but a fresh, new medium ready for magic.

When cleansing fabrics with the Air Element, I prefer to hang the materials outside on the line to dry. If that isn't a viable option for you, use the dryer instead. Whichever choice you make, call upon the Spirits of Air, saying:

Oh fresh clean Air, which blowest free
Dry this fabric of fibrous blend
Harken to what I ask of thee
Your freshness to this spell, please lend.

Visualize the breeze blowing through every thread of the fabric, whisking away undesirable vibrations.

After the cloth is dry, iron it well so that you can work with it more easily. As you iron, visualize the heat further searing away negative vibrations and invoke the Spirits of Fire, saying:

Oh heat of fire, these fibers smooth
Press the wrinkles from them now
All bad vibrations, please remove
No negativity allow.

Keep in mind that preparing the materials for magical use is as personal an endeavor as any other type of magic, and that the guidelines presented above are simply suggestions. If something I've suggested doesn't feel right, change it to fit your personal needs. In order for magic to be effective it must be dynamic, so spread your wings and fly a little bit. Feel the enchantment, experience the magic, and soar into your own personal realm.

Magical Sewing

Assembling the Magic

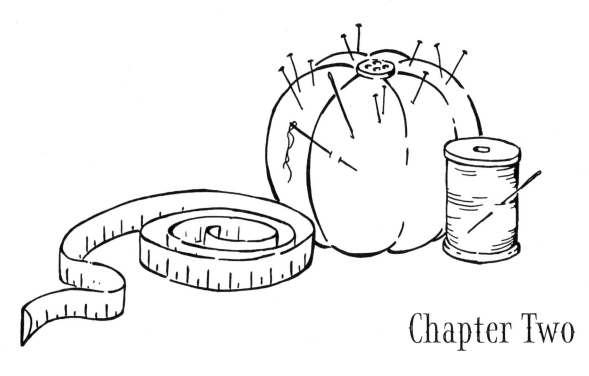

Chapter Two

A wealth of superstition, folklore, and augury surrounds sewing. For example, in some areas of the world, the wives of fishermen refuse to tend woolen thread after sundown for fear they will soon sew their husband's burial shrouds. Perhaps the most common superstition regarding the process comes from an old adage familiar to almost everyone: "See a pin and pick it up, and all the day you'll have good luck. See a pin and let it lie, before the evening you will cry!"

The basis for this adage is fact and very logical. Prevention of an accident is lucky, and a pin on the floor is an accident just waiting to happen. Left to lie, it is sure to wind up in someone's foot. Just the same, I've picked up pins in the street and chuckled happily as my luck began to change right before my eyes. Luck is luck—no matter the cause—and whether the basis is fact or folklore is immaterial.

Threads and pins don't hold the monopoly on sewing-related prophecy, for needles and scissors have long held their own in foretelling that which is to come. For instance, if a needle breaks in two while sewing by hand, it ensures good fortune, while a needle that breaks into three pieces foretells an offer of marriage. Needle breakage while sewing on a machine signifies the receipt of good news regarding money from a distant relative. (Of course, breaking a needle while sewing may just indicate that you're using the wrong needle for the job, and it is doubtful you will receive any money for that!)

Another superstition says that a gift of scissors must be reciprocated by a token coin or the blades will cut the friendship. Dropping scissors—an act which I used to think signified clumsiness—is prophetic, too. If someone makes a wish while a pair of dropped scissors

sticks into the ground, it supposedly comes true. The number of points that stick in the ground and the days on which the implement falls are also significant. One point announces a death and two points announces a marriage. Scissors that fall from the hand on Sunday indicate a strange visitor, but if they drop on any other day of the week, it means that the workload will increase by leaps and bounds.

Because so much superstition surrounds the practice of sewing, it is likely that our ancestors also found it to be a magical practice. Folklore seldom lies where magic has not roamed.

Letting the Fabric Choose You

That which might be considered odd on the mundane level is perfectly normal on a magical level. The act of choosing a crystal or stone for magical work is an excellent example. Seldom does the practitioner choose the stone; the stone most often chooses the practitioner.

This sort of thing happens to most practitioners at one time or another. We find ourselves in a shop that we normally would not have entered, looking at a stone that really doesn't appeal to us, yet draws us like a magnet. We buy the stone and later discover that it is the perfect tool for a particular ritual or for a friend in need of its properties.

The same is usually true of choosing fabric for magical projects. I am often drawn to a particular piece of fabric although I don't know its purpose. There are times that I even know the precise yardage to buy. Years ago, I would have thought this a silly whim and refused to make such a purchase. Today I follow my instincts and buy whatever supplies I seem to need. Sooner or later, the Ancients always show me what to do.

Learning to trust the subconscious takes a bit of practice, but it is a skill worth mastering and definitely pays off when it comes to magical sewing. Listen to your intuition and you will never be sorry.

How Does Your Energy Flow? Considering Fabric Design and Texture

When I walk into a fabric shop, I have to resist the urge to touch every bolt in the store. I find that I'm not alone in this predicament. Fabric texture is magical and certain textures invoke deeply emotional responses. Because of this, textures are important when choosing fabric for magical use.

Just like stones, colors, incenses, and herbs, different textures have different energies. Consider the type of energy flow necessary for the magical project you have in mind. Should the energy flow unobtrusively and smoothly in a continuous motion? Would an assertive energy that rises to a peak, then levels out be better? If you were going to sew a dressy outfit to calm a hyperactive child, for instance, a smooth, silky fabric might be most magically effective. A thick, nubby tweed would more than likely defeat your purpose, because that texture lends itself to activity. Listed here are a few types of fabrics with textural guidelines for magical workings.

BROCADE is a perfect fabric to use for prosperity spells and financial gain. It smacks of royalty, riches, and plenty.

CORDUROY is much like velvet in magical vibration, but because of the ribs in its weave, more activity is present. Use corduroy when immediate, rather than gradual, change is necessary.

COTTON fabrics such as percale, calico, voile, oxford cloth, broadcloth, and poplin are smooth and passive in texture; they are useful for spells requiring a soft touch. Those cottons with a nubbier feel—such as piqué, terry cloth, chenille—have an active textural vibration. Cotton fabrics are suitable for any spellworking, but the energy of this fiber is more subtle than that of other appropriate fabrics.

EYELET can be used in magical workings intended for joy, happiness, and youthful pleasures. The "eyes" also give added protection against the evil eye.

FELT is another fabric that has superb properties of insulation. I recommend felt for almost any magical project, because it holds the energies of enchantment beautifully. It is an excellent choice for poppets and magical supply cases, and because it does not ravel, much of the finish work normally required in sewing is unnecessary. Felt usually comes in solid colors, but embroidery or beadwork may be added to create active vibrations for any spell.

HOMESPUN fabrics bustle with activity, but the thick-and-thin quality of the texture is also excellent to use in sealing relationships of every kind. Its qualities include tenacity, endurance, and strength.

LINEN has a crisp texture that makes it useful in efforts requiring quick and definite change. There is nothing subtle about the feel of linen. Use fine handkerchief linen when working with complicated transitions; it helps in smoothing away difficulties. Nubby, suit-weight linen (especially in black) works beautifully for efforts involving quick and painless separation.

SATIN is very soothing to the touch and promotes the qualities of beauty, harmony, and peace of mind.

SILK provides a strong, insulative fabric. Because shantung and douppioni are nubby, their textures are active, while the energies of smoother silk fabrics, such as charmeuse and China silk, are fluid and passive in personality. Because it was originally intended for cocoons, silk fabric is an excellent choice for efforts involving protection.

TWEED is a fabulous texture to use when a project requires a lot of activity. It is excellent for boosting energy—magical, creative, physical, and so on.

VELVET is a good choice for workings involving love and romance. Though its texture is smooth, the nap of the fabric lends itself to motion. This fabric brings warmth to any project. It is terrific for efforts involving smooth change, making it an excellent choice for breaking bad habits.

WOOL fabrics come in a variety of textures and, like silk and felt, hold the property of insulation. The protective vibrations of wool are looser than those of silk. Wool allows positive energies to flow in while holding negative energies at bay. For projects requiring a soft touch, try wool crepe or challis. A thicker fabric used for outerwear, such as melton or gabardine, is more useful in efforts where heavy protection is an issue.

Fabric pattern is just as important as texture, for the pattern often depicts built-in symbols. Printed and woven-in patterns vibrate toward activity, while solid colors relate to a slow, deliberate, and fluid motion. Go ahead and use calico for passive projects if your intuition moves you to do so. Although I find solid colors better suited for passive endeavors, a small, evenly distributed, and unobtrusive print may prove very successful for some non-aggressive projects.

Never discount synthetic or synthetic-blend fabrics for magical use. Polyester, for example, literally means "many esters." The "esters" that combine to form polyester are fibrous strings of plastic that can be bonded to natural fiber to add strength. Many polyester fabrics incorporate recycled plastic. Polyester is available in many textures. Employing synthetics within the scope of your magical project does not hinder the spellworking, and can help clean up the environment. What could be more magical than that?

Scissors, Pins, Needles, and Notions Set the Magic into Motion

Fabric selection aside, perhaps the most important task in any sewing project is pinning and cutting out the pattern. Make sure that the cloth is free of wrinkles and that the arrows marked on the pattern pieces lie in the direction of the fabric grain, otherwise the finished seams will refuse to lay flat and no magic in the world will make them behave. As you pin the pattern pieces in place, chant something like:

> Little pins of steel and light!
> Hold each piece with strength
>   and might—
> Pierce the fiber in and out—
> And infuse with magic 'round about!

Any tailor or seamstress will tell you that a sharp pair of scissors is imperative for successful sewing, because a clean cut along the pattern line is a big help in straight seaming. (Incidentally, scissors bear sacredness to Kali the Destroyer.) Carefully cut out the pattern pieces one by one, enchanting each by saying:

> Oh tool of sharpness, tool of steel!
> Form these pieces of my spell.
> The edges of their shapes, please seal,
> So they will fit together well!

When the pieces are pinned and snipped to shape, you are finally ready to sew. It is a good idea to enchant the first stitch of every step of any magical project, so as you begin, try this chant or one of your own construction:

> Oh piercing needle, that which gleams!
> [Your intention] is the reason for this
>   spell.
> Weave its purpose through these seams,
> And bind it thoroughly and well!

To Go High-Tech or Knot

The most overlooked magical needlecraft tool is the sewing machine. With a magic all its own, the machine interlocks two threads as the needle moves up and down through the cloth, making a perfect representation of the union of the God and Goddess. This interlocking action strengthens seams, which in turn adds strength to the magic. Because the machine's stitches are straight and evenly distributed, magic flows in a more focused, even stream. A tool devised of many tiny parts that move in perfect harmony toward effectiveness could be nothing less than magical.

So, what about knot tying and focus? A tug on the top thread of a machine-sewn seam brings the bobbin thread through to the surface, and leaves a means of tying any knots needed for enchantment or binding. Focus can be maintained with a simple chant that corresponds to the purpose of your project. For example, when working on a project for financial prosperity, you might chant something like:

> Money come and fill my pot!
> Increase the wealth with every knot!

Sewing by hand is magical, too, and guiding the needle as it pierces the cloth is a terrific way to focus on a spellworking. In handsewing, knot tying takes on a slightly different feel; because the needle needs threading more often, there is more opportunity for sealing magic into the project. The following chant works well for me:

I bind this portion of my spell
With steel and fiber, tied so tight.
Hold these handmade stitches well,
Contain their magic and their might.

Handsewing takes longer and though going a bit slower is sometimes better for me, it may not be better for you. Magic—especially needle magic—is a very personal craft. Do whatever feels right for you, make your own magical decisions and use your imagination, for deviation from the "norm" is what separates the mundane from the magical.

What's Sew Magical? Giving Mundane Articles Magical Flavor

Driving cross-country several years ago, I missed a turn and happened across a tiny occult shop. If I hadn't gone in to ask directions, I would have missed learning of a magical form that at the time was foreign to me. The store was decorated with a multitude of handmade rag dolls. After talking to me for a while, the owner finally admitted that she wasn't a doll collector. The dolls were spirit dolls, designed specifically to protect the shop, its owners and employees, and the positive vibrations in the atmosphere.

Each doll had its own personality, function, and reason for living in the store. One sat on the cash register to protect the money and bring new customers, some kept watch over the shop and its contents, and others absorbed any scattered or negative energy in the spellcasting and reading rooms.

Further conversation with the owner revealed that spirit doll magic worked very well for her. Though burglars plagued neighboring businesses, no one bothered the shop. She went on to say that people who normally would never venture into the neighborhood flocked there for readings and supplies. The shop continued to flourish, although bankruptcy loomed over many other businesses in the area.

Doll magic doesn't have to stop with the actual dolls, though. Their clothes can be enchanted as well. Kausalaya of San Anselmo, California related a story about giving Chandra—a doll with a magical wardrobe—to her Goddess-daughter as an introduction to the Sabbats and the realm of spirituality.

One of Chandra's outfits is a robe covered with gold stars, suns, and a blue Earth. Chandra wears it as High Priestess of the Solstice Coven. She has a leaf-brown gown for the Samhain Circle and a Lucia gown for calling back the Sun's light. There is also a lion costume, because her class celebrates Earth Day and she speaks for the lion.

Each outfit has a be-ribboned note attached to explain its enchantment. For example, a winter coat of simulated Persian lamb's wool acts as a lesson in animal rights. The attached note reads: "This is my fur coat. Of course it's only make-believe fur—the Goddess Mother says, 'Real fur only belongs on the critter that grew it!'"

A special blessing charm of thread ends accompanied Chandra to her new home. The attached note gave her new friend instructions to leave the charm outside in the spring so the birds could use it to build their nests.

The number of sewing projects you can imbue with magic is limitless. Magical endeavors that immediately come to mind are ritual robes, altar cloths, amulet bags, and cloth covers for the Book of Shadows.

What about instilling magic in ordinary sewing projects? Items such as fabric dinner napkins and placemats may be charged to lend a feeling of warmth and welcome to all who use them. Spells to alleviate fear and to promote courage may be stitched into clothing for a child's first day of school. Camouflage clothing for the hunter may be dedicated to Diana and consecrated specifically for safety and success. A handmade stuffed animal could be blessed with protective qualities and used as a guardian for the home or for a child's room. Slip covers, curtains, dish towels, tea cozies, and basket cloths are all mundane projects that will allow themselves to be enchanted. The list is endless—if you can sew it, you can spell it.

Some basic sewing knowledge is necessary to complete the sewing projects given in this chapter. For example, you must know what a selvage is, how to find the fabric grain, and be able to work some simple stitches such as a whip stitch, blind stitch, overcast stich, and slip stitch. If these terms are not familiar to you, try one of the books in this chapter's suggested reading list. Failing that, pick up a needlecraft magazine at your local newstand or supermarket. Nearly all of them have a general instructions section that contains this information.

Fairie Blouse or Dress

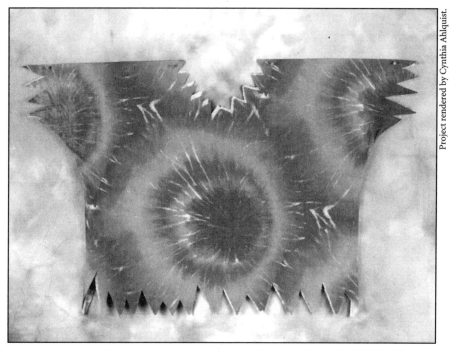

Project design by Susan M. Baxter of Crafts for the Craft from Starwood.

Make this festive outfit for Midsummer Night's Eve and dancing in the moonlight. Light a pink, yellow, or white candle and burn floral incense to strengthen the merriment. Ask for guidance, play some dancing music, and let your spirits fly. Adorn this outfit with beads, paints, embroidery, ribbons, little flowers, or whatever your heart desires.

Materials

1½–2 yards light weight India gauze for blouse

2–2½ yards lightweight India gauze for dress

fabric glue, fabric paint, or an assortment of beads with large holes (optional)

fabric dyes (optional)

NOTE: Be sure to use the India gauze, otherwise the blouse or dress will not drape and flow properly.

To Make the Blouse or Dress

Dyeing the Fabric

If you choose to dye the fabric, do so before sewing the outfit. You will need the following:

old toothbrush and small section of wire window screen

or

soft paint brush and rubber bands

Pick a color to suit the kind of fairie you want to be—pastels or brights for flowers; greens, oranges, golds, and browns to blend into the woodland; or blues for water. For multiple tones, tie dye, spatter dye, or watercolor dye the fabric before you cut and sew.

Tie Dyeing

To tie dye, gather the washed fabric in random places and tie off with rubber bands. Dip the fabric in an accent color and allow to dry. Remove the ties and radiating areas of the original color remain.

Spatter Dyeing

Spatter dyeing works well with thickened dye, a toothbrush or soft paintbrush, and a piece of wire window screen. On a still day, hang the fabric on a clothesline after washing and let it dry. Dip the toothbrush into the dye and wipe off the excess. Then hold the wire screen near the fabric and make small spatters by flinging the brush toward the screen. For larger spatters, use a paintbrush without the screen.

Watercolor Patterns

Achieve a watercolor pattern by hanging wet fabric. With a two to four-inch paintbrush, paint on one or more dye shades in large quick strokes, and allow it to run down the fabric. Use a spray bottle of water to make the colors run evenly.

Sewing the Blouse or Dress

When the fabric dries, cut out the blouse or dress. Fold the fabric to suit your taste for length in front and back, then fold it again length-wise so that the shorter length faces the

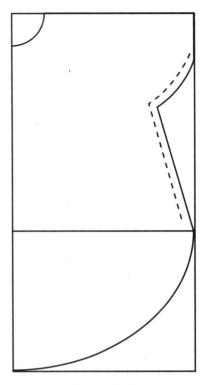

FIGURE S-1.

outside (see Figure S-1). My top reaches the hip bones in front with a slightly shorter center, and the center back falls to the knees. For the dress, cut the front about knee-length and the back long enough to brush the ankles.

Cut a curving line first, then sew the side seams, cutting the ragged edges last. Cut curved edges for the sleeve, the front, and the back. Trim the neckline lower on the front side and higher on the back side.

Unfold the fabric, putting the sides of the front and back together and the right sides of the fabric together. Sew the sleeve and side seams together as shown by the dashed lines in Figure S-2 (following page).

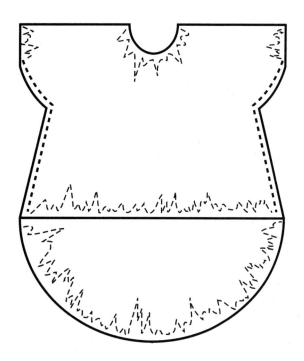

FIGURE S-2.

Cut the bottom in random ragged edges as shown in Figure S-2. (A pinking shears works well for this.) You can leave them raw, but they get more ragged with time and eventually, the garment will fray. If your prefer, sew, embroider, or bead the raw edges.

You can also go over the edges with squeeze-on fabric glue or paint. For painting or gluing, use a large cardboard box covered with foil or plastic. Pin the fabric edges to the box with large straight pins. Paint or glue the area pinned to the box, let dry, un-pin, and then move the fabric over until all the jagged edges are sealed.

All-Purpose Poppet

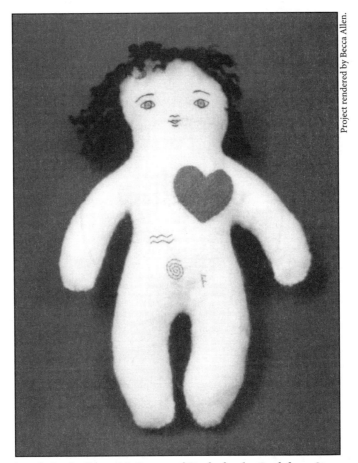

Project design by Susan M. Baxter of Crafts for the Craft from Starwood.

Project rendered by Becca Allen.

Poppets are magical tools that help bring a specific result to a specific person. Full Moon is an excellent time to begin this project, but as emergencies must be met, this poppet may be constructed at any time. Remember: **never** make this for anyone without his or her permission. Don't neglect making one for yourself, because you deserve the blessings the poppet brings, too.

Materials

1   12" x 12" square of felt to match skin color

    sewing thread

    sewing and embroidery needles

    cotton balls or fiberfill for stuffing

    herbs, incense, and candle appropriate to the purpose

    taglock of the person for which the poppet is intended (a bit of hair, fingernail, et cetera,) embroidery floss or fabric paint to match eye and lip color

yarn to match hair color

small scrap of felt in the appropriate heart color (green or blue for healing, pink for love, yellow for creativity, purple for psychic guidance, et cetera.)

an article of old clothing from the individual the poppet should represent (if this is not possible, a piece of paper on which you can write may be substituted)

Poppet pattern.

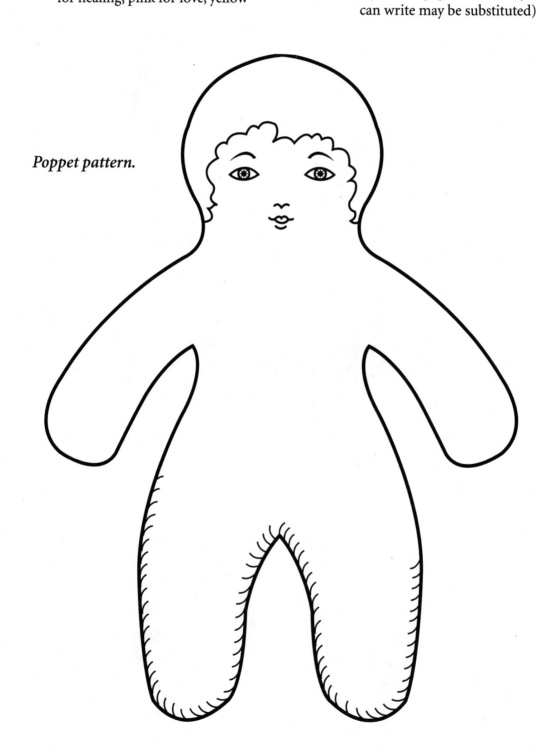

To Make the Poppet

Before you begin, put on some inspiring music and clear your mind of everything but the intention of the project. Light the incense and the candle.

Begin by folding the felt in half and transferring the pattern to the fabric. Cut out the pieces, thinking of and visualizing the person and the desired outcome. Wrong sides together, overcast the edges in small stitches. Chant the person's name over and over and stuff the extremities with fiberfill or cotton as you go. If an illness resides in a specific extremity or organ, place the herbs in that location as you stuff.

Place the taglock (along with a small crystal or stone if you desire) in the center of the body. As you work, chant something such as:

Make _____ whole!

or

Bring _____ healing.
(or peace, love, et cetera)

Embroider or paint on the hair and face, as well as symbols and identifying marks. (See Appendix A for stitch patterns of astrological, planetary, and other magical symbols.) Sew a heart to the poppet.

If some of the person's old clothing is available, wrap the poppet inside. If not, write the person's name on a piece of paper and tie it to the poppet with an appropriately colored ribbon. Ask the deity of your choice to assist you in the intended purpose.

Herbal Protection Charms

Project rendered by Cynthia Ahlquist.

Project design by Anteia of East Hampton, New York

Try these charms of protection to safeguard your home, family, and friends from all negative energy and unsavory beings.

Materials

4" x 4" squares of white or blue fabric

Herbs

Small amounts of the following:

balm of Gilead

hyssop

myrrh

rue

unpeeled garlic cloves

rosemary

mugwort

To Make the Charms

Right sides together and leaving one side open for turning and stuffing, seam the squares of cloth while chanting:

> **My power as a Witch**
> **Goes into each stitch**
> **Guarding well from harm**
> **All who use this charm.**

Turn the bag right side out, stuff well with herbal mixture, and sew the top shut. Scatter the charms in every room of the house and give them to everyone you love.

Velveteen Star Pin Cushion or Ornament

Project design by Susan M. Baxter of Crafts for the Craft from Starwood.

Project rendered by Kitty Laust-Gamarra.

See a pin and pick it up, all the day you'll have good luck.

See a pin and let it lie, before the evening you will cry.

Everyone knows that it is bad luck to walk by a pin without picking it up. It is considered so unlucky that in Essex this rhyme was quoted as a warning. This velveteen star with Victorian flavor is a fabulous project for keeping pins in order. Because of the association of pins with luck, visualize a surge of good fortune, success, and the power of the star entering your life as you work on this project. (This star may also be used as a window or Yule tree ornament.)

Materials

¼ yard velveteen fabric

   pinking shears (use instead of scissors, as velveteen frays easily)

   sewing and beading needles

   fiberfill stuffing, cotton balls, or old pantyhose

1 8-millimeter round gold or silver bead

   glass beads (seed and bugle) of your color choice

   embroidery floss and needle (optional)

To Make the Velveteen Star

Photocopy the star pattern (below). Using the photocopy as a pattern, cut two stars from the wrong side of the fabric with the pinking shears. Leave a ½ inch between the two, so that when you cut them out, you can add the necessary ¼-inch seam allowances. Right sides fac-ing, sew the stars together, leaving an inch or two open for turning. As you stitch, seal your luck and success by chanting:

> **Luck be sealed and bane begone —**
> **As I stitch around this star,**
> **Bring success and fortune's song!**
> **Good luck abound from near and far!**

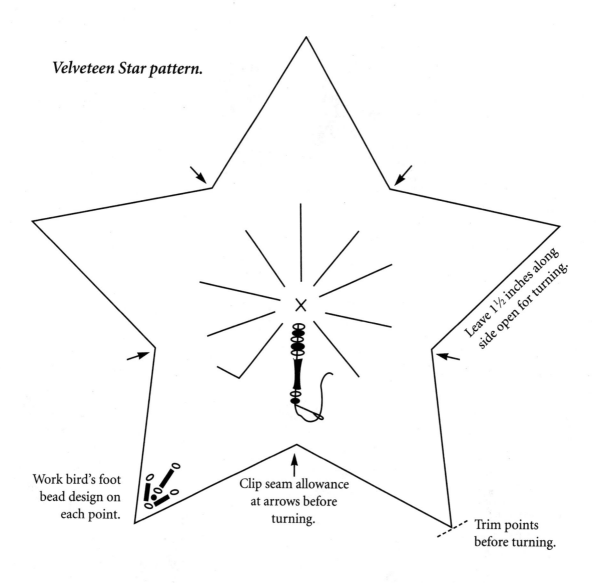

Velveteen Star pattern.

Leave 1½ inches along side open for turning.

Work bird's foot bead design on each point.

Clip seam allowance at arrows before turning.

Trim points before turning.

Clip the seam allowance close to the stitching at the arrows, being careful not to clip past the stitching line, then trim the seam at the points of the star. Turn the star right side out, stuff firmly and slip stitch the opening closed.

Find the center of the star and with the beading needle and thread, stitch back and forth several times through both layers of fabric at the center to pull the layers of fabric together. Sew the large bead in the center, and keeping the bead placement in mind, slide the needle through the center of the pincushion to the beginning of each line in turn. Pick up the seed and bugle beads with the beading needle, then slide them down the thread. Pierce the fabric and bring the needle out at the end of the next line. Stitch a tiny bird's foot design in the corner of each point (see pattern).

To make a hanger for the star, thread six strands of embroidery floss through a needle. Pierce the top of the star, bring the thread length half way through the fabric, and remove the needle. Tie the floss ends in a knot or bow.

Tool Holders for the Magical Needlecrafter

Project design by Susan M. Baxter of Crafts for the Craft from Starwood.

This set of needlework cases is ideal for the magical needlecrafter. Not only do they keep your supplies handy, they also insulate the tools from negative vibrations.

Materials

1 12" x 12" square of felt (purple is good for protection)

  embroidery floss and needle

  glass seed beads (optional)

  moon and star sequins (optional)

  stuffing—fiberfill, cotton balls, old pantyhose, sawdust, thistledown, or the silk of milkweed

2½ yards ¼" satin ribbon

  small felt scraps of various colors

  a large safety pin or jewelry pin

  beading needle (optional)

To Make the Tool Holders

Burn a candle and incense to help raise your creative energy flow.

Pin Cushion

Cut two circles of felt from the pattern on the opposite page and embroider the moon and star designs on one or both pieces. Accent with beads or sew on moon and star sequins. As you work, chant something like:

New Moon Beginnings
Cycle New,
Bring creativity
To make this true!

Blanket stitch the two pieces together with embroidery floss, but leave an opening for stuffing. Cut a length of ribbon, fold it in half to form a loop, and pin the ends to the inside of the pin cushion. Stuff, then finish closing with the blanket stitch, being sure to catch the ends with the stitching.

Scissors Case

The scissors case fits four-inch scissors. If that is too large or small, make your own pattern by tracing around your scissors and leaving some extra space at the sides to accommodate their thickness.

Cut one full piece of the pattern (shown on the following page), one piece from the tip

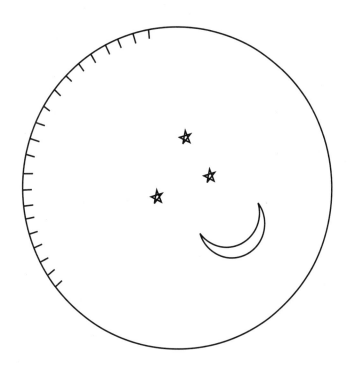

Pin cushion pattern.

to the top of the ribbon line, and two extra tips for reinforcement.

Embroider on or sew sequins to what will be the outside of the flap and bottom of the case. Visualize the scissors always at hand and sharp, chanting something like:

Scissors sharp,
Scissors true,
Always near,
Cut like new!

Attach a strip of ribbon to hold the flap down. After folding the flap over, attach a loop of ribbon at the top of the case for hanging. (The top dotted line on the pattern shows approximately where to fold.) Pin the two extra reinforcement tips to the inside of the case, then blanket stitch around, starting at the flap holder, continuing around the tip, and finishing at the other side of the ribbon strip.

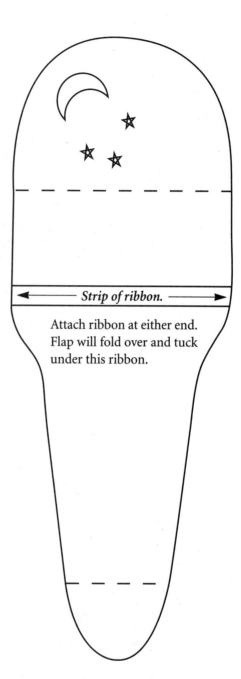

Strip of ribbon.

Attach ribbon at either end. Flap will fold over and tuck under this ribbon.

Scissors case pattern.

Needle Case

The needle case is two layers thick; the inner layer is smaller than the outside (see needle case pattern below). Cut out both pieces and embroider on or sew sequins to the front of the outside layer. As you work, chant:

> **Case of fabric!**
> **Stars and Moon!**
> **Keep my needles**
> **Sharp and true!**

Fold the inside layer in half to find the center, then on one side cut two horizontal slits about ¼ inch apart and ½ inch long to hold the needle threader. Center the inside layer on top of the outside layer and blind stitch the two together. Cut two 3½-inch lengths of ribbon and attach one to each of the outside edges for tying the case shut, then sew a ribbon loop to the top of the fold line for hanging. Pass the needles through a ritual candle flame while you hold them with pliers and chant:

> **Needles sharp**
> **Needles new (old)**
> **Make my stitches**
> **Straight and true (bold)!**

You may wish to do something similar with new pins for the cushion. At any rate, pass all of your implements through the smoke of incense to bless them. Attach all ribbon loops to the safety or jewelry pin.

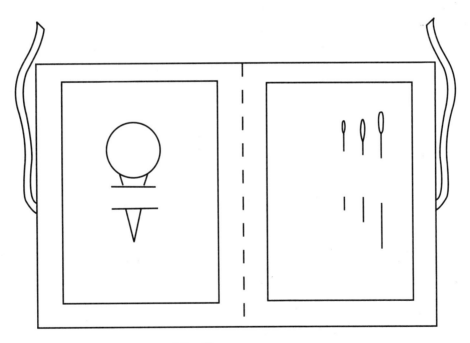

Needle case pattern.

A Helping Hand, a Magical Hand

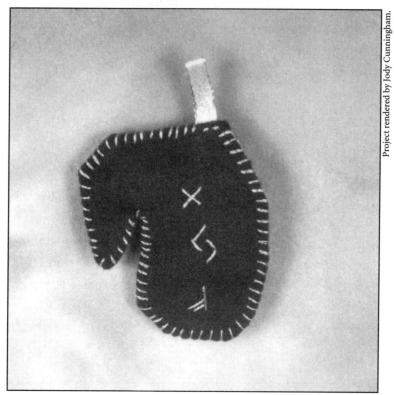

Project rendered by Jody Cunningham.

Project design by Susan M. Baxter of Crafts for the Craft from Starwood.

This little charm is easy, cute, effective, and non-Pagans won't even guess what it is. The best time for construction is at the new Moon, and it may be embroidered with runes and symbols for any purpose.

Materials

- appropriate candle
- appropriate incense
- 2 small felt scraps (at least 3" x 4") in an appropriate color
- embroidery floss and needles
- appropriate herbs
- appropriate stones
- 3" piece of ¼" ribbon for loop

To Make the Helping Hand

Light the candle and incense and ask your deity to aid you in making the charm for your specific need. Cut two mitten shapes from the felt (see the pattern on the opposite page), while chanting an appropriate phrase or verse. For instance, if you are making the charm for prosperity, you might chant:

Scissors slice through felt with speed!
Bring money now to fill my need!

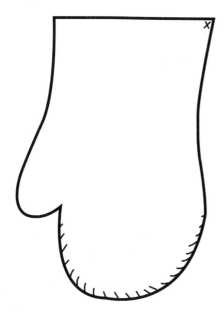

Helping Hand pattern.

Embroider the symbols on the front mitten. The following are some suggestions.

Love

These are excellent for attracting the love you deserve! Use pink felt, rose petals, rose quartz, and the following runes and symbols.

Prosperity

Make this charm of green felt, gold, or silver thread; a penny; a green stone; nutmeg; and the following runes and symbols to attract money and increase your finances.

Strength

If you lack vitality and energy, make this charm from red felt, a bay leaf, tiger's eye or banded agate, and the following runes and symbols.

Protection

Make this charm for children. It is an excellent talisman to hang in their rooms. For its construction, use white felt, lavender, hematite, and the following runes and symbols.

Leaving the top open, overcast the two pieces together while chanting:

Needle stitch these pieces well
Bring fruition to this spell!

Fill the mitten with herbs and stones. Chanting the verse above, close the top of the mitten with overcast stitches and sew a loop of ribbon in the upper, right hand corner.

Place the charm on your altar for nine days; burn an appropriate candle and incense for nine minutes each day while meditating upon the purpose of the talisman. On the tenth day, anoint the mitten very lightly with an appropriate oil and carry it on your person until full Moon. Then add the fertile energy of the Earth by burying the charm in the ground. (Don't forget to leave an offering of food or coin for the Earth Spirits.)

Witch Spirit Doll

Project rendered by Dorothy Morrison.

Project design by Dorothy Morrison.

Spirit dolls may be made from any purchased doll pattern or one of your own design. The pattern itself is unimportant; the enchantment with which you fill the doll is what makes it effective.

One of these little witch dolls was given to me by my dear friend, Barb. "Naomi" lives on a corner shelf in my kitchen-dining room atop an earthenware pot made by my son. Because Naomi's seams were completely sewn shut when I received her, I filled the pot with lavender and cinnamon, and added a chip each of rose quartz and amethyst. This mixture protects the area from negative energy while promoting unconditional love—a good combination of vibrations for a place where so many of my friends and loved ones congregate.

Because making this project from scratch allows total access for stuffing, try placing an appropriate herb/stone mixture within the figure itself.

Materials

- ⅜ yard black or black print fabric
- ¼ yard muslin
- small amount of fiberfill
- 5" piece of jute or frayable rope
- black, fine-line, felt-tip marking pen
- cotton swab
- red, felt-tip pen
- 1 small scrap black felt
- glue gun and hot glue sticks
- embroidery needle
- 2 yards crochet thread or twine
- 1 cup of wild birdseed
- herbs and stones to suit your purpose

To Make the Witch Spirit Doll

Decide upon the doll's purpose, then cut out the pieces (see the pattern pieces on this and the following pages), adding a ¼-inch seam allowance to each. Right sides together, seam the legs, leaving the top side open. Turn the legs inside out and stuff the feet with a small amount of fiberfill, then tie a knot in each leg just above the foot. Fold the arm piece lengthwise so that both raw edges meet in the center and press down with an iron, then fold it in half lengthwise and press again. Stitch close to the edge on the right side and tie a knot in the center of the piece.

Center and baste the raw edges of the legs to the right side of the dress piece (turn the feet upward toward the neckline area). Then right sides together, sew the shoulder, sleeve, side, and bottom seams of the dress, leaving the neckline and sleeve edges open. Turn the piece inside out and fold the neckline area under so that it is even with the shoulder seams. Turn ¼ inch under at the sleeve edges and press.

Sew the head/body pieces together, leaving the bottom open. Turn inside out and stuff with fiberfill. Center the piece of jute on top of the head and secure it well with stitches, then

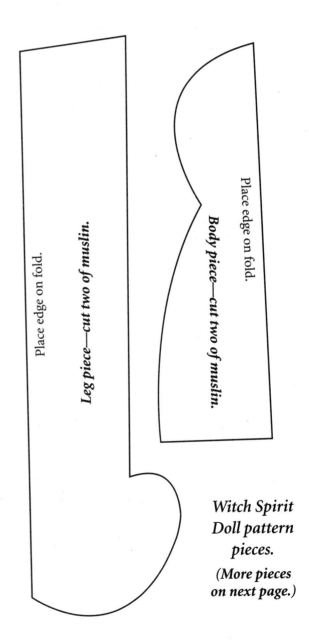

Place edge on fold.

Leg piece—cut two of muslin.

Place edge on fold.

Body piece—cut two of muslin.

Witch Spirit Doll pattern pieces.
(**More pieces on next page.**)

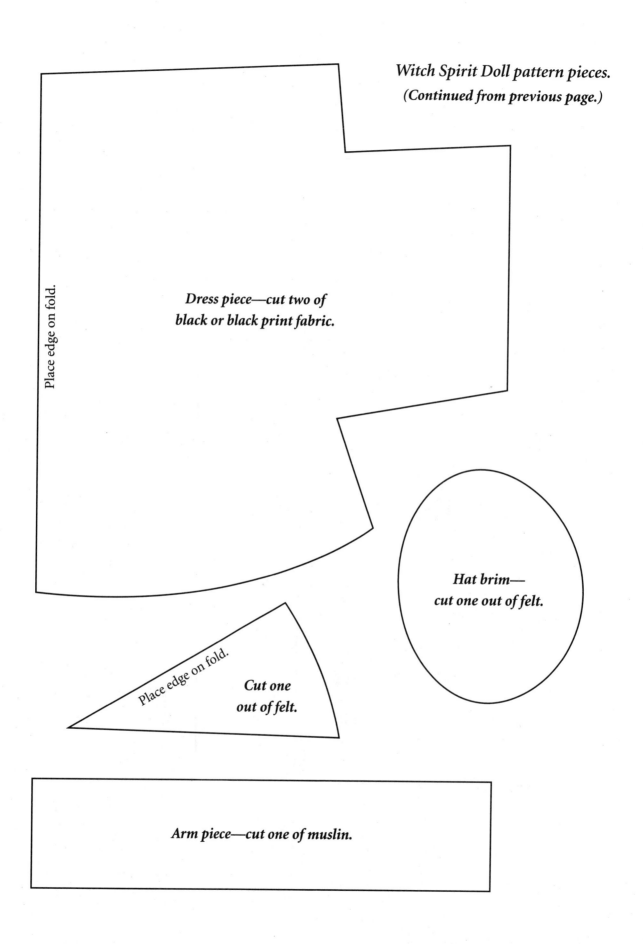

Witch Spirit Doll pattern pieces.
(Continued from previous page.)

Place edge on fold.

Dress piece—cut two of
black or black print fabric.

Hat brim—
cut one out of felt.

Place edge on fold.

Cut one
out of felt.

Arm piece—cut one of muslin.

fray out the jute, separating every strand. Draw the face on the doll with the black marker. For cheek color, dampen a cotton swab with water, "bleed" some of the red marker on the tip and apply it to the face.

Sew the back seam of the felt cone and turn it inside out. Hot glue it to the hat brim, then carefully hot glue the hat to the top of the doll's head.

Pin the raw ends of the arm piece to the inside of the sleeve openings so that the knot is on the front side of the body. Using the embroidery needle and cotton crochet thread or twine, take running stitches around the sleeve openings, making sure to secure the arm piece as you stitch. Remove the needle, draw up the ends to gather and tie in a small bow. Repeat the process with the neck area, but leave the thread ends loose.

Concentrate on the purpose of the doll for a few minutes, visualizing precisely what task you wish it to perform. Pour the birdseed into the dress/body of the doll and mix in the herbs and stones you wish to use, chanting as you work. If you wish to enchant your spirit doll for the purpose of protection and love, you might chant something like:

With these herbs and stones I give you life!
Protect this place from stress and strife!
Promote kindness, joy, and harmony!
Go to work [name of doll]! Blessed Be!

Insert the head/body piece firmly into the seed/herb/stone mixture, then draw up the neck thread ends tightly around it and tie into a bow.

Suggested Sources for Specialty Fabrics

Dharma Trading Co.
P.O. Box 150916
San Rafael, CA 94915
(800) 542-5227

Free catalogue available.

Garden Fairies Trading Company
P.O. Box 5770
Santa Rosa, CA 95402
(707) 526-5907

Send $4 for catalogue and fabric swatches.

Gohn Brothers
Box 111
Middlebury, IN 46540
(219) 825-2400

*Send fifty cents for current price list
and catalogue.*

Mekong River Textiles
8424 Queen Anne's Drive
Silver Spring, MD 20910
(301) 589-1432

*Send $1 for current catalogue
and more information.*

Mini-Magic
3675 Reed Road
Columbus, OH 43220
(614) 457-3587

Send $5 for current catalogue.

Suggested Sources for Alternative Patterns

Ms. Susan Baxter
Crafts for the Craft of Starwood
9736 N. Hassetown Road
Morgantown, IN 46160

*Send a self-addressed, stamped envelope
for a full list of patterns and projects.*

InaRae Ussack
Craft/Crafts Magazine
P.O. Box 441
Ponderay, ID 83852

Magical

Patchwork
and Quilting

Piecing Together the Magic

Chapter Three

Patchwork exhibits every basic principle of creation—destruction, conception, and birth. In order to create, one must destroy. Such is the way of patchwork. Cut fabric into pieces and you ruin its original form. Move the pieces around, match them up differently, and you conceive a new idea. Stitch the pieces together and before you know it, new life bursts forth with fresh form and pattern.

There is a lot more to the magic of patchwork than the initial creation process, though. Magic thrives and grows within the vibration of each pattern piece. The energy of each individual shape figures in, numerology has its place, and color vibration plays an important role. This artform also enables the practitioner to work with every magical symbol imaginable. Magically speaking, there is no more perfect medium than patchwork.

Geometrical Patchwork

Most patchwork patterns come from the interaction of four geometric shapes: squares, rectangles, diamonds, and triangles. These figures are angular and indicative of male energy. Let's look at their symbologies for a moment.

SQUARES consist of four sides of equal length and four right angles. They can symbolize the four seasons or the four suits of the Tarot. Numerologists tell us that the four is the number of organization, solidity, and duty. Squares resonate dependability. Use them as a grounding force for your magic.

RECTANGLES also consist of four lines but vibrate differently than the balanced square. Because two sides are short and two sides are long, they do not provide the same uniformity. Instead, they tend to radiate a "holding" energy equivalent to the bars on jail cells. For this reason, rectangles make excellent magical binders. These shapes also work well in patchwork if the object of your magical project is to shield or to guard. Use them for protection magic, to fend off harm or sickness, or to keep a loved one safe.

DIAMONDS are angular shapes with slanted lines and a unique vibrational energy. Though this shape isn't round, it may be used effectively to represent the Wheel of the Year—the sides being the Quarter Days, and the points being the Cross-Quarter Days. Diamonds also work well in any type of prosperity magic, from the shape's association with the marquise cut stone of the same name. The shape is airy, symmetrical, and perfectly harmonious; it works well to instill those vibrations in any magical project.

TRIANGLES call to mind the power of the pyramid. They make good symbolic representations of the Triple Goddess or Triple God. Imagination, expression, and inspiration belong to this shape, as well as mastery, good fortune, and optimism. Because the triangle is representative of the creative force within, it makes an excellent addition to any magical patchwork project.

Free-Form Patchwork (Crazy Quilting)

Free-form or crazy quilting is another form of patchwork. It is one of the most magical types of pieced work because there are no boundaries to contain the creative effort. The kaleidoscopic design runs rampant, wild, and free in a collage held together by helter-skelter stitchery.

A good portion of the magic that vibrates from this type of patchwork comes from the bonding of the specific fabric pieces and trims. Traditionally, the crazy quilt comes from fabric scraps gathered from friends and family, with no two pieces being alike. Today, the materials used in these quilts often come from old clothes that have special meaning to the needlecrafter or to the person for whom the item is made.

Free-form patchwork is a wonderful way to preserve a family history or build a personal testament that may be passed down through future generations. Such a venture could record a particular period in someone's life or even commemorate a single unforgettable day. The magic of crazy quilting lies not only in its boundless creative potential, but also in the vibrational energies left by the people who once cherished the materials. These energies live on long after the original owners. What could be more magical than that?

Curved Patchwork and Appliqué

While some work is pieced from angular shapes, other patchwork patterns are curved and indicative of female energy. Working with curved patchwork takes more concentration than piecing geometrical patterns, so the focus necessary for smooth shaping makes it ideal for magical needlecraft projects.

Like geometrical patchwork, curved pieced work forms a patterned block. Unlike geometrical patchwork, though, curved work relies heavily on easing the shapes to fit. Sometimes a gathering stitch is necessary, and getting the seams to lie flat often takes a little practice.

Appliqué is a design cut out of fabric and sewn on top of another piece of cloth. Appliqué allows design freedom unavailable in geometrical patchwork. It enables the practitioner to incorporate virtually any type of symbol into a project—hearts, flowers, leaves, acorns, grape bunches, and more. Hand appliqué can be somewhat time-consuming. Machine appliqué takes less time, because it only requires a tight zig-zag stitch around the edges of the shape. Because the art of appliqué allows for a wide range of symbolism, it is well worth the effort to perfect its techniques.

Usually, curved pieced work employs four basic shapes: circles, three-sided cones, four-sided cones, and inverted cones, which sometimes form a block corner. Like geometrical shapes, the rounded figures of curved work carry their own vibrations and symbologies.

Circles, though seldom used in patchwork, hold much meaning for those on the magical path (Figure PQ-1). Frequently used to represent the Goddess, they also symbolize the magical Circle; the cycle of birth, death, and rebirth;

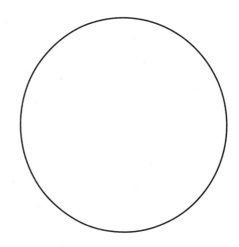

FIGURE PQ-1.

the Wheel of the Year; and the cycle of Nature. The circle offers vibrations of smoothness, continuity, immortality, and it is the most feminine of the basic shapes used in patchwork design.

More often, though, the three-sided cone (Figure PQ-2) takes the place of the complete circle, because sewing several of these shapes together forms a circular pattern. The three-sided cone retains some of the triangular energy of the pyramid, but is softer and gentler. Like the triangle, this shape vibrates toward creativity, but the curvature at its end causes the creative force to flow more smoothly. Inspirational energies also belong to the three-sided cone, making it a wonderful device for invoking the powers of the Muses.

The four-sided cone (Figure PQ-3) represents balance and duality, the perfect harmony of yin and yang, and the perfect union of the male and female forces.

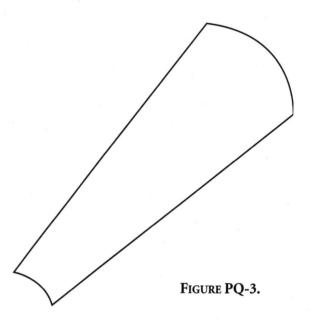

FIGURE PQ-3.

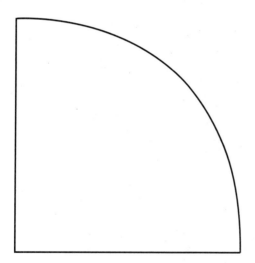

FIGURE PQ-2.

The inverted cone (Figure PQ-4) looks like the three or four-sided cone except that the top curves inward. Depending upon the position of this shape, it may be used to represent the power of either the waxing or waning Moon.

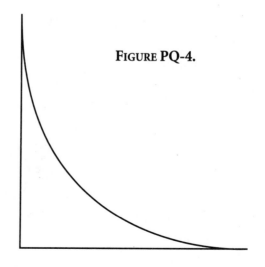

FIGURE PQ-4.

Magical Patchwork and Quilting: Piecing Together the Magic

Because shapes pieced together may take on completely different vibrations when joined to form a design, many factors figures into choosing the perfect pattern to fit your magical needs. Remember that a shape or design that symbolizes a certain energy or magical form to you may hold an entirely different connotation to someone else—and there is no right or wrong symbology within the realm of magical patchwork. What is important is the way in which you view the overall picture and the concentrated intent with which you work.

The following are a few patterns that hold magical significance for me. If none of these ideas strike your fancy, explore the design realm a bit more fully. Check out the public library, your local arts and crafts store, or follow your intuition and construct your own magical pattern. Who knows? You may design a pattern that continues to live long after you have reached the warmth and luxury of the Summerland.

Magically Symbolic Patchwork Designs

Pandora's Box

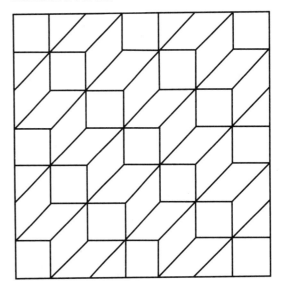

Even the name given to this design has a magical ring. Two diamonds and one square form each section of the design, giving the overall illusion of a three-dimensional box. Worked in white, red, and black, it represents the Maid, Mother, and Crone aspects of the Triple Goddess and is an excellent design for asking the Lady's blessing or protection.

Eight-Pointed Star

Rolling Star

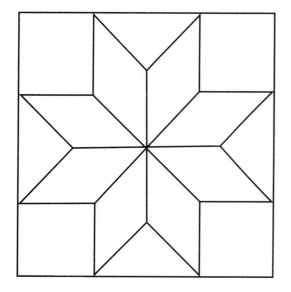

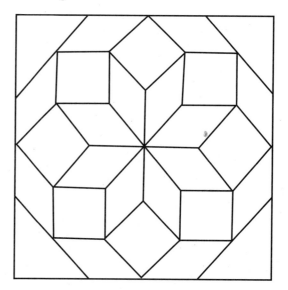

An unknown artist devised this patchwork design late in the seventeenth century. It rapidly gained popularity with the early American settlers, and by the time of America's first centennial, thousands of variations of this pattern were in circulation. Sacred to Ishtar, the eight-pointed star is an excellent tool for invoking the energies of the Goddess and for symbolizing the eight Sabbats or the Wheel of the Year.

A variation of the eight-pointed star, this design can be very symbolic when viewed with the magical eye. When working with this design, I use the center star to symbolize the eye of the Goddess, with the four vertical and horizontal blocks and the four diagonal blocks representing the Quarter Days and the Cross-Quarter Days, respectively. The diamonds that encase the design and tie it together symbolize the turning of the Wheel of the Year. Depending on the colors chosen, the triangles that make up the four corners may be used to represent the four seasons, the Triple Goddess, the Triple God, or the Elements.

Flying Swallows

Incorporating squares, triangles, and diamonds, flying swallows is a perfect design for symbolizing the consummation of the marriage between the Lord and Lady. When piecing this design, I cut the small triangles from white to symbolize the Goddess in Her Maiden aspect, and the diamonds from green to represent the Green Man.

Spools

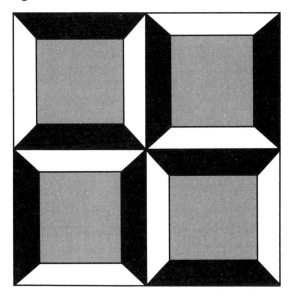

What patchwork design could hold more personal enchantment for the magical needlecrafter than spools? It depicts four spools of thread pieced together in a block—pointing East, South, West, and North. Not only does this design provide excellent symology for boosting creativity, but it is also a perfect representation of the balance of the Elements. To use it as such, cut the background pieces of purple or white (symbolizing Akasha) and the squares of "thread" from yellow, red, blue, and green.

Texas Star

Nine Patch

The Texas star is the only commercial patchwork design in existence that forms a perfect pentacle. As pentacles have an association with coins and money, this design works well when used for prosperity rituals. For most of us, though, the symbology of the pentacle runs much deeper as it symbolizes our religion, the macrocosm of humanity, and the mind in conjunction with the forces of Nature. This design also works beautifully in efforts of blessing or protection.

I doubt that any patchwork design is more more magically symbolic than the nine patch, for no other number is as firmly ensconced in magic, mythology, science, and superstition than the number nine.

For instance, nine times any number aside from zero always numerologically reduces back to nine (2 x 9 = 18 and 1 + 8 = 9, and so on). Traditionally, magicians cast a nine-foot Circle because of mathematical correctness; after all, a circle equals 360 degrees and 3 + 6 + 0 = 9. Nine planets grace our solar system, the nine Muses bestow creativity and inspiration, and a cat is said to be lucky to have nine lives.

Use the nine patch design to boost your magic, creativity, luck, and focus on planetary workings.

Grandmother's Fan

Seven Dancing Sisters

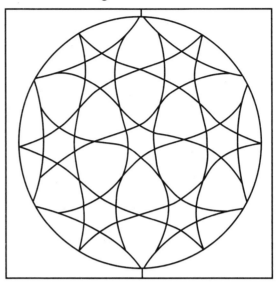

The six "spokes" joined to a quarter circle in this design resemble a hand-held fan. Worked in shades of pink and rose, it vibrates toward love and harmony and works well in gifts for newly handfasted/married couples. This design also has a hidden symbolism, for by stitching together the inner seams of four pattern blocks, it changes to form a circle and all that the circle symbolizes. (The circular design is commonly known as winner's circle.)

Steeped in ancient mythology, this design depicts the Pleiades—a small cluster of stars located in the constellation of Taurus—encased within a circle. The names of the individual stars in the Pleiades come from the names of the transformed daughters of Atlas and Pleione: Alcyone, Celaeno, Electra, Maia, Merope, Asterope, and Taygeta.

Because this design holds seven stars within a circle and the number seven bears an association to Saturn (the planet of karmic lessons), it could symbolize protection and guidance from the Lady as we learn our personal lessons in this lifetime. The design might also be very symbolic to those who make their living on the open sea, for astronomy and navigation sail side by side.

Numbers and Blocks and Magic! Oh My!

Figuring the number of blocks and pattern pieces necessary for the finished product is an important part of planning any patchwork project. To get an accurate count of blocks, divide a side measurement of the finished block into the number of inches required first in width, and then in length. Then multiply the number of blocks in the width by the number of blocks in the length for the total sum of blocks necessary. For example:

96" [finished width]
divided by
12" [12" x 12" block]
= 8 blocks

108" [finished width]
divided by
12" [12" x 12" block]
= 9 blocks

8 x 9 = 72 blocks

To determine the sum of a particular pattern piece necessary to finish the project, count the number of pattern pieces used in a block, then multiply that figure by the number of total blocks.

6 [pattern piece A]
X
72 [total blocks]
= 432 pattern piece A

Sometimes a magical patchwork project requires a bit more calculation. Because you know which magical vibrations you want to transmit, planning a magically and numerologically correct number of blocks is critical to the energies. Occasionally, joining the correct number of blocks presents a dilemma to the magical needlecrafter, because the finished project may end up larger or smaller than necessary. To rectify such a problem, trace the pattern pieces onto graph paper and enlarge or reduce the shapes until they form a block of adequate size.

Each digit has its own unique energies. A quick look at these will aid your planning.

ONE. This number belongs to the self. The number of the magician in the Tarot, it evokes imagination in conjunction with the inner power. Use this number to invoke your creative power and bring your goals to fruition.

TWO. This is the number of relationships and may be used to represent the duality of Godhead, the male/female forces, the mind's effective changes upon the Cosmos, or even a business partnership. It may also be used to represent sharing, interaction, and balance.

THREE. This digit belongs to friendship. Use it to signify laughter, celebration, strength, and fortitude. Because the number three is symbolic of the Triple Goddess, Triple God, and the Laws of Karma, it works well to represent these, too.

FOUR. This is a very protective number and can be used to represent safety, good health, good luck, and psychic well-being. It is an excellent number to use if you seem to have a lack of organizational or communication skills as well, for the number also belongs to Mercury.

FIVE. Not only is the number five connected with the properties of the Elements, it simply exudes energies of prosperity; thus, it may be used to represent abundance, financial comfort, and plentiful harvest. It is also the number of the student and its vibration is useful for the retention of knowledge.

SIX. This is the number of happiness, love, and harmony. Use this number when working projects for family endeavors, newlyweds, children, or those who can't seem to find the joy in life.

SEVEN. Because karmic lessons belong to the realm of seven, this number may be used for any effort concerning reincarnation, wisdom, the elderly, or the Ancients. Use it, too, to ease the pain of karmic lessons.

EIGHT. This number relates to the Wheel of the Year and the changes in the Earth. Whether planetary or personal, this number works well for any environmental endeavor. It is also a good number to use for change in lifestyle, change of habit, or change in fortune.

NINE. Sacred to the Goddess, the number nine is especially effective for efforts involving magical attainment. It belongs to the psyche and is an excellent choice for ritual construction, spellcasting, or even seeking out your spirit guide. It is also a good number for prophetic dreaming and divination purposes.

The index of numerological values stops here; numbers of larger values reduce to the single digits already listed.

This is all well and fine if you don't need more than nine blocks for a project, but what if nine blocks will not quite suit your purpose? Simply determine which magical properties you want to instill in the project and plan the effort using that number of blocks across and down. If that isn't feasible, use two different numbers and incorporate the vibrations of both. For instance, if you plan to make a quilt for a pair of newlyweds but a formation of six blocks by six blocks is too wide, try working a combination of five blocks by six blocks. After all, a bit of financial prosperity wouldn't hinder the happiness of a couple just on the brink of a new life. (Besides, 5 x 6 = 30 = 3 = friendship; 5 + 6 = 11 = 2 = partnership.)

Setting the Magic in Motion with Templates, Pencils, and Scissors

Before getting too involved in a magical patchwork project, you might find it helpful to sketch a colored layout of the finished effort. This gives you a general idea of what the project will look like, and whether proposed color combinations will yield the desired effect. (For help with magical color themes, see Appendix B in back of this book.)

It is also a good idea to take the time to construct a sample block before buying fabrics for the project. This gives you a chance to check the feasibility of a patchwork design and more closely figure the necessary yardage.

Making precisely cut patterns or templates is important when preparing to stitch a sample block. The easiest way to handle this process is to place a sheet of clear template plastic (available at most arts and crafts stores) over the pattern pieces and trace the pattern markings onto it. A piece of tracing paper works well, too, and may later be glued to lightweight cardboard to add some body. No matter which method you use, pay attention to whether the patterns have seam allowances marked on them. If they don't, make a notation to add a ¼ inch seam allowance around the edges, so you will remember to add it when you transfer the markings to the fabric.

Because transferring patchwork patterns to fabric is somewhat different than working with sewing patterns, here are a few tips which might come in handy:

1. Construct a sample block from unbleached muslin. It is lightweight and easy to sew by hand or machine.

2. Lay the fabric out smoothly without folding it, and transfer the pattern to the wrong side of the material. Make sure that the arrows on the template are in line with the grain of the fabric.

3. Use a sharp pencil for tracing around the templates. This allows for cleaner, more precise lines.

4. Mark the seam allowance and stitching lines clearly on the fabric. This step ensures that all the seams meet correctly.

5. Press the seams open as you stitch. Ironing the seams prevents puckering and makes work lie flat.

Stitch the sample block, examine it carefully, and then consider the following: Do the seams meet properly? Does the design lie flat? Would a heavier or lighter fabric work better for the design? Make a few notes, as they will come in handy when considering fabric and texture types.

To arrive at a ballpark figure of the necessary yardage, mark the areas of the block you plan to piece with colored fabric. For example, if the design calls for four three-inch, green, right (ninety degree) triangles per block and you plan to use sixteen blocks for the finished project, multiply the amount for one block (four) by the amount of blocks necessary (sixteen) to get the total sum of the required triangles (sixty-four). As most fabrics suitable for pieced work are thirty-six inches wide, figure how many pieces may be cut from the width (twelve).

Divide the number of necessary triangles (sixty-four) by the number that may be cut from the width (twelve). Round off that figure to the next highest number to determine how many inches of fabric you need for that part of the project. In this particular case—assuming that the three-inch form includes the seam allowance—eighteen inches or a half yard of thirty-six-inch-wide green fabric is sufficient for the triangles.

Following this process for each pattern piece will give you a fairly close idea of the fabric amounts to purchase. The calculations out of the way, gather the fabric, piece the spell, and set the magic on its path.

Quilting: Layering the Magic

Quilting is a beautiful artform that has much in common with the basic dynamics of magic. Not only are both crafts handed down generation to generation, they are often worked in a group in a formation called a circle. Both require special tools and strict adherence to ritual preparation. The repetition involved is often monotonous and beneficial to meditation; moreover, that same repetition causes an end result many people call magic.

Yes, quilting is a very magical art. Its foremost qualities are harmonious connection and unification. The stitching interlocks the layers into one solid piece.

There are two basic types of quilting: stitched and tufted, each with its own secondary properties.

Tufted Quilting

Tufted quilting is done by drawing both ends of a sturdy thread through the layers and back again to the first side of the layers, then knotting the two ends. As all knots are a form of magical binding, this technique can be used to seal the enchantment of a patchwork pattern or the color vibration of a solid color quilt. The number of knots the magical needlecrafter uses in each tuft might further denote its magical intent; that is, six knots for love and harmony, nine knots for wishes, and so on.

Stitched Quilting

Stitched quilting can carry all magical properties, because the stitching design may be drawn to represent any magical symbol the quilter prefers. One might stitch dollar signs or clover on a prosperity quilt, hearts and flowers on one for love, or stars for healing and protection. The following are a few standard quilting designs that hold magical symbols.

Stitched Quilting Designs That Mirror Intent and Purpose

Diagonal

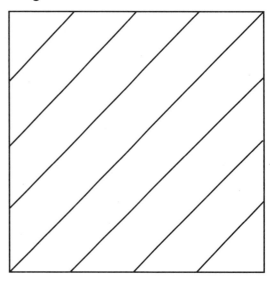

The diagonal quilting design is magically versatile. For instance, lines running from the lower right corner to the upper left can represent Air, and lines travelling from upper right to lower left create a symbol of Water. Sets of stitching lines crisscrossing from corner to corner represent the solidity of Earth, while lines that originate at the upper corners and make a point in the center can symbolize Fire. Lines that form a V-shape with the point facing upward are an excellent representation of protection and blessings bestowed upon us by the Lord, the Lady, and the Ancients.

Straight

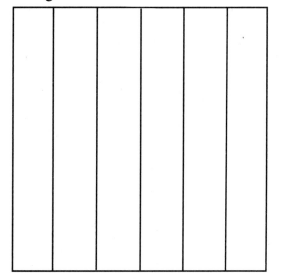

"Straight as an arrow," "The straightest path from Point A to Point B," and "straight shot" all come to mind when looking at this stitching design. It represents the paths travelled on both the mundane and spiritual planes. Try it, too, for speedy but effective solutions to difficult problems and for efforts related to hunters or warriors.

Clam Shell (also known as Teacup and Baptist Fan)

The rounded stitching of the clam shell design is indicative of the smooth feminine motion of Goddess energy and is a wonderful design to employ when asking favors or blessings of the Lady. It is also excellent for invoking the energies of the sea or for changing the tides in your life.

Cable

The fluid curve of the intersecting cable design is reminiscent of ancient Celtic knotwork. It represents harmonious connections, relationships, and the intertwining properties of love. It works well on borders as a means of sealing those magical vibrations into a project.

Feathers

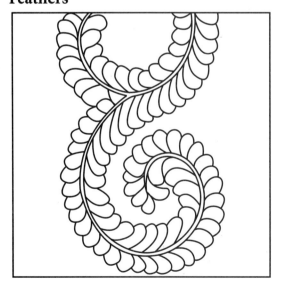

The most beautiful common quilting design is feathers. It symbolizes lightheartedness, joy,

and happiness. Use it on projects to overcome depression, to more easily change a bad habit, or to ease trauma.

Overlapping Circles

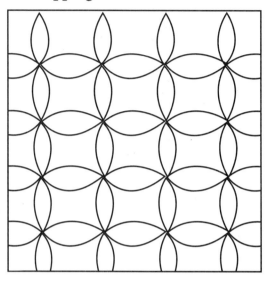

This stitching design consists of many circles that overlap each other by one-fourth. Because the circular shapes interconnect, this pattern may be used to symbolize the cycle of life; however, because the intersections form an inner four-scalloped edge in each circle, this pattern may also represent the magical Circle and Quarters or the Elements.

Crescents

Use this quilting design to call upon the boundless energies of the Moon. It is most effective in efforts involving divination, psychic power, or general magic.

Wine Glass

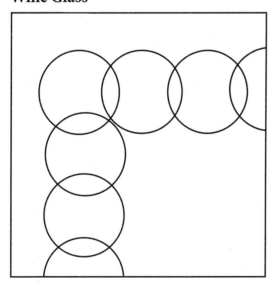

This design consists of a square within a circle. It represents yin and yang, good and evil, the balancing effect of the Elements, or the effect of the four seasons upon the Earth.

Interlocking Links

This stitching design resembles the path impulses travel to reach the brain. Use it in efforts designed to quicken the thought process, to increase memory retention, and to achieve clarity of mind.

Squares

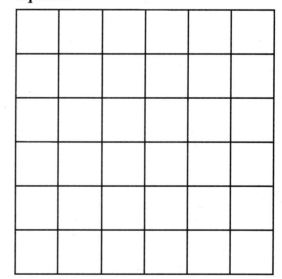

Just as the circle represents the Goddess, so the square symbolizes the God. Use this design in efforts to invoke Him or any energy of a strong and rugged nature. Squares are also work well in protecting from negative energies.

Quilting By the Piece

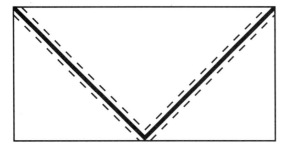

To quilt by the piece, simply stitch along the seams formed by the patchwork design. The magical properties of this technique are sealing, binding, and strengthening. Use it when you wish to reinforce the magical properties already present in your project.

There are no rules for choosing a quilting design for your magical project. On a magical level, intricate designs reflect activity and rapid change, while the simpler ones represent slow and deliberate motion. For example, you might wish to embellish a healing project with an extremely lavish design in order to bring about a quick recovery. An effort intended to bring a new attribute into your life might be better suited to a simple diagram, so as to make the change steady and gradual.

Some practitioners prefer to construct a quilting diagram of their own instead of using a market standard. If you would like to make your own template, first draw the design on a piece of cardboard and cut it out. Place the template on the quilt top and trace its outline on the fabric with a quilter's pencil. (The drawing remains on the fabric during the stitching process, but magically disappears after a quick swish through soap and water.)

Stitching the Layers Binds the Magic

A quilt is a sandwich of three pieces: the top (often patchwork), the batting or "filler," and the backing (Figure PQ-5). To prepare the "sandwich" for quilting, place the backing face down, the batting on top, and the quilt top right side up over the other two. Smooth the wrinkles from the pieces, pin them together from the center out, and baste them together as shown.

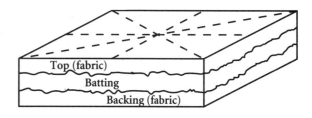

FIGURE PQ-5.

Place the sandwich in a quilter's hoop or frame to keep the layers wrinkle-free while you work, then begin stitching in the center of the piece and work outward. Working from the center prevents unsightly puckers and keeps fabric stretch to a minimum. There is also a magical reason for stitching in this fashion. All magic begins at the center (the practitioner) and flows outward. Quilting in this way tells the Universe to get ready for the magic and help it on its way.

Most quilters use short needles called "betweens" for their stitchery. Betweens work well because they are sharp and just the right length for piercing quilt layers. Basically, the quilting process is a simple matter of bringing the needle up and down through the layers while using the diagram lines drawn on the quilt top as a guide.

Here are a few tips that might help you with the quilting process:

1. Quilting is tedious to the eyes as well as the fingers. Be sure to work in adequate light—the brighter, the better.

2. Hide first stitch knots by bringing the needle up through the layers and giving the thread a quick tug. This brings the knot up from the underside and hides it in the batting.

3. When stitching along the diagram, take small and even stitches. This ensures the proper shape and outline of magical symbols, while adding a harmonious vibration.

Although quilting is not difficult, it is time-consuming. To pass the time and keep the magical state of mind intact, try listening to music in tune with the intent of the project. Chanting as you stitch works well, too. Regardless of your method of choice, remember to concentrate on the magical intent of the project as you stitch—strong focus adds power to the enchantment.

After stitching, secure the raw edges of your project with wide seam binding. Unfold the seam binding and lay it wrong side out on top of the patchwork top, then pin it all the way around the project. If the piece of binding is too short, seam another piece to it. Carefully miter the corners. (See the package directions for easy ways to miter.) Stitch the binding securely to the edges, remove the pins and then fold it over the edge of the quilt. Complete the process by whipstitching it down on the back side. As you bind the edges, you may want to chant something like:

Bind enchantment with these seams
Bind the magic, bind the dreams
Seal the spell and be it done
By Earth, Wind, Sea, and Shining Sun!

When working with a magical patchwork or quilting project, remember that it is magical and that the rules that pertain to the physical plane seldom apply to the realm of enchantment. Don't hesitate to deviate from any guidelines or add personal touches, even if you are unsure of the purpose. Know that there is a reason for everything within the realm of magic; consistently relying upon your instincts lets your magic sprout and blossom.

Some basic patchwork and quilting knowledge is necessary to complete this chapter's projects. For example, you must know what a selvage is, how to find the fabric grain, and be able to work some simple stitches, such as whip stitch, blind stitch, and slip stitch. If these terms are not familiar to you, try one of the books in this chapter's suggested reading list (page 81). Failing that, pick up a needlecraft magazine at your local newstand or supermarket. Nearly all of them have a general instructions section that contains this information.

Harmony-in-Your-Life Patchwork Heart

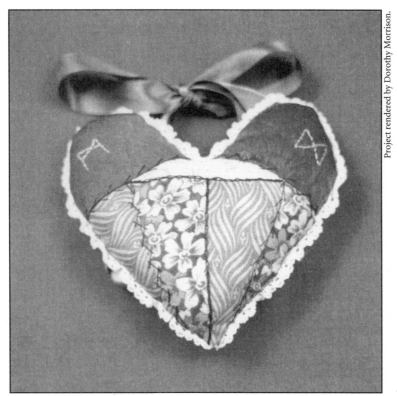

Project design by Dorothy Morrison.

Life today takes on a much faster pace than it did in days gone by. There never seem to be enough hours in the day and everyone is in a constant hurry. If you work outside the home, chances are that you rush through morning traffic knowing that your in-basket is overflowing with paperwork. There are meetings to attend, the computer is down, and the printing you needed yesterday won't be ready until next week. Your boss insists you leave town for a weekend business trip, knowing full well that it is your anniversary and you have special plans with your spouse. Your secretary just called in sick, the phones are ringing off the wall, and the temporary agency just announced that they have no one available.

Working inside the home is no better. There are beds to make, children to dress, meals to cook, and dirty laundry to wash. The phone rings just about the time you are thoroughly up to your elbows in dirty dishes, and you learn that your in-laws are planning to visit—first thing in the morning. You are late for the fundraiser meeting, and as you rush out the door, you realize that your dog has the postal worker's pants leg in his jaws.

We have all been in these types of situations. They are stressful and disconcerting, and, left unchecked, can cause ferocious anxiety attacks. It is enough to send you running to your psychoanalyst's office. Before you pick up the phone to make an appointment, try this magical project. It is wonderful for when you feel out of balance and unable to handle any more stress.

Materials

- 1 piece of sturdy cardboard or posterboard for template
- craft knife or scissors
- 2 10" x 10" squares of unbleached muslin
- small red or rose fabric scraps
- small fabric scraps in harmonizing colors
- embroidery floss (optional)
- 1½ yards ruffled eyelet or lace
- 1 yard ¾" ribbon
- small portion of polyester stuffing (two pairs of old pantyhose may be used instead, if you like)

To Make the Patchwork Heart

On a piece of cardboard, draw a symmetrical heart a bit larger than you would like the finished project to be. Cut it out with scissors or a craft knife and put it aside. Arrange the fabric scraps collage-style in an overlapping fashion on one of the muslin blocks, making sure that you cover the entire block.

Pinning as you go, turn under the visible raw edges to the pieces still overlap. Sew the pieces to the muslin, using a blind or slip stitch, so that the stitches will not show. As you sew the bits of fabric to the block, concentrate on the pieces of your life harmoniously fitting into place—one portion joining to another just as the fabric does on the muslin.

Add desired qualities or vibrations to your life by embroidering appropriate stitches on the connecting fabric lines. For instance, you might work a series of yellow cross stitches for joy or pink and rose interlaced running stitches for balanced love. (For more ideas, check the next chapter on magical embroidery.)

Trim any excess colored fabric from the muslin and pin the unused block (right sides together) on top. Center the heart on top of the blocks and trace around it. As you cut out the heart, concentrate on removing from your life anything that is disconcerting or troublesome.

With the right sides of the hearts together, pin the lace between the two so that the straight edge is even with the edges of the cloth, and the ruffle lays inside. Cut the ribbon in half and insert the lengths between the two hearts, pinning an end to the center of each upper curved area. Starting at the bottom of the heart and taking ¼-inch seams, sew the hearts together, sealing harmony and balance into your life with every stitch you make. Leave an opening for turning and stuffing. As you turn the heart inside out, know that your life is being "turned around" as well, and that perfect harmony and balance are replacing stress and strife. As you stuff the heart, chant over and over:

I fill my life with laughter!
I fill my life with love!
I fill my life with harmony
And sunshine from above!
I fill my life with sanity!
I fill my life with ease!
I fill my life with clarity
And joy and hope and peace!

Slip stitch the opening, tie the ribbons into a bow, and hang.

The Neophyte's/Initiate's Coverlet

Project rendered by Dorothy Morrison.

Project design by Dorothy Morrison.

This is an excellent project for those walking the spiritual path of Paganism or Wicca, and a delightful way to be mindful of the lessons successfully learned along the way. The coverlet is a lengthy magical project, but one of the most powerful I have ever encountered. How long it takes to finish this magical effort depends upon how long it takes you to complete each level or degree of your path. The student makes one block of the blanket at the completion of each lesson, symbolically representing the knowledge gained or the mystery revealed. It is difficult to give specific directions for this project, as the subject matter of lesson plans vary with each tradition.

Materials

assorted colors of fabric for blocks (usually ¼ yard of each color used is more than enough for any particular block)

a piece of fabric as large as the finished project to be used for the backing (if this is not plausible due to the width of the coverlet, then purchase twice the amount of the project length)

an assortment of thread to match the fabric colors

a piece of batting as large as the finished project (apply the same rule as used for the backing, if you are not able to obtain a piece with the correct width)

several packages of quilt or blanket binding (or extra wide seam binding—enough to equal the total distance around the finished coverlet, plus 2 to 3 inches for joining)

A Sample Coverlet

In my tradition, the level of Neophyte contains thirteen lessons. Though it might seem exasperating to design a quilt top with thirteen blocks, it is really not that difficult.

One solution might be to plan the layout in three rows of three, with the last four lesson blocks taking the form of wide patchwork strips that frame the first nine. I planned my quilt top around a large center block, which I bordered with twelve smaller ones (see photo, above). If your degree plan has an odd number of lessons, just invoke your imagination. With minimal effort, you can design a beautiful quilt top that is not only meaningful, but fits together perfectly.

The neophyte lessons in many traditions are multi-faceted. Though each one covers practical information, magical theory, magical exercises, Element and tool workings are also included. If such is the case with yours, do not be overwhelmed. Choose a particular portion of the lesson and plan a block around that theme.

For example, a block design for a lesson on the Elements could begin with a center square of purple or white to represent Akasha (see Block 4). A strip each of yellow, red, blue, and green could be stitched to the edges in a clockwise fashion to symbolize Air, Fire, Water, and Earth. A lesson on wand making could take the form of an appliqued block depicting a tree branch to symbolize the tree you befriended, a coin to represent the gift you offered, and, of course, the finished wand. Chakra lessons might require a simpler block and be represented best by piecing together strips of the chakra colors with each strip in its respective order.

For general idea purposes, the blocks I used in my coverlet are listed here with their symbolism. Figure PQ-6 (opposite page) shows which blocks of the coverlet are which. Some blocks are blatantly informative while others are much more subtle in nature. When choosing design blocks for your personal coverlet, remember that there are no rules. All that matters is that you remember the lesson when you see the block.

Block 1	Block 2	Block 3	Block 4
Block 12			Block 5
Block 11	Block 13		Block 6
Block 10	Block 9	Block 8	Block 7

FIGURE PQ-6.

Courthouse Steps (Block 1)

This block represents the personal path. Even though every path leads to the center of the Universe, each one is as different as the person who travels it. This block reminds me that no single path is right for every person, and that I must be tolerant of those whose paths differ from mine.

Intertwining Moons (Block 2)

Though the Moon is usually indicative of the Goddess, in my coverlet, this design represents all deities. The white background symbolizes Their impact on my personal world.

Card Trick (Block 3)

This block symbolizes cause and effect, and karmic balance. With its intersecting placement, this design reminds me that everything I do affects not only my life but also the course of someone else's. I must live my life with care so as not to upset the karmic plan or the lessons it lays out for us.

Crazy Quilt (Block 4)

The crazy-quilt portion of this block signifies the turmoil from which all creativity is born. The frames that border the block bring it order, harmony, and direction. This reminds me that I am the magician and have control of my own life no matter how chaotic the circumstances may seem. It also tells me that there is a solution to every problem. All I have to do is sit back, take a deep breath, and look at the total picture.

Baby Blocks (Block 5)

This block represents the concentration and focus required for effective magic. As symbolized by the lower three blocks, all magic begins with a culmination of ideas. The center blocks remind me that all unnecessary and unrelated ideas must fall away to give the magical act shape and form. The top block symbolizes the perfect melding and intertwining of the ideas and energies, and the focus necessary to channel them into physical manifestation.

Fence Rail (Block 6)

This block symbolizes the perfect balance necessary to live effectively in both the spiritual and physical worlds. When we achieve this, both worlds come together as represented by the strips that form the block center.

Log Cabin (Block 7)

This block symbolizes the Elements. For further information, see the block ideas above and the stitching instructions below.

Appliquéd Heart (Block 8)

The heart in the center of this block symbolizes perfect love. The background diamond, surrounding triangles, and frames remind me that this sort of love is always based on perfect trust.

Eight-Pointed Star (Block 9)

There are many eight-pointed star designs in existence, but I found this one to be most symbolic of the Sabbats and the Wheel of the Year.

Nine Patch (Block 10)

As indicated by its name, this block represents the number nine, the number of wish manifestation. It reminds me that, through personal magic, I have the power to change my own reality and achieve my innermost desires.

Stained Glass Tulip (Block 11)

Even though tulips are a part of the plant world, in my coverlet, this flower symbolizes all of Nature. The stained glass "leading" in this block is representative of the harmonious human interaction with Nature that is necessary for effective magic and successful living.

Hidden Circle (Block 12)

The center sphere of this block represents the Ritual Circle, the world between the worlds. The patterned shapes forming the Circle border symbolize the Element Guardians that lend their energies to divide the worlds and hold the power within the Circle.

Pentacle Block (Block 13)

This block represents my initiation into the Craft. While the star symbolizes the spiritual realm, the patterned arches indicate the physical connection that must be present for effective, powerful magic. The background circle that encases them signifies my acceptance into the coven, and the personal support of each member there. The Nine-Patch border denotes the initiation ritual itself, and the four-pointed stars in each corner are a stylized representation of my magical tools (cup, wand, pentacle, and athame).

To Make the Coverlet

Stitching each block should be a magical ritual in itself. To better focus on the block's lesson, try chanting something related to its teachings. After piecing all the blocks, offer the coverlet to the Lord and Lady and the Ancients for Their blessing. You may use this blessing or one of your own construction.

> **Oh Gracious Goddess of the Night**
> **And Fiery Lord of Light of Day**
> **I offer you this symbol of**
> **The knowledge gained of ancient ways**
> **Please bless this symbol of the path**
> **I walk in perfect trust and love**
> **Please help me learn Your Mysteries**
> **Within, without, below, above!**
> **So Mote It Be!**

Place the batting under the finished coverlet and cut it to size. (If you were unable to purchase it in the correct width, cut two pieces of batting to the proper length, lay them side by side and sew them together by hand using an overcast stitch. Then cut the piece to size.)

Using the top and batting for a pattern, cut the backing fabric. If the fabric is not wide enough, handle it the same way as the batting, except for joining. Instead, join the two pieces using a straight stitch and ½-inch seam allowance. Pin all three layers together. Quilt this project by the piece, then seal the raw edges with seam binding.

Magical Soap Bags

Project design by Dorothy Morrison.

We have all the seen the "take-me-away" bath oil commercials and identified with them. Because of the stress of today's busy lifestyles, the bath has become not only a means of physical cleansing, but also a prescription for relieving tension, calming the mind, and general unwinding. Herbal baths can temporarily relieve the mind that won't be still, sore and achy muscles, and morning sluggishness. It can also relieve less mundane ailments such as a lack of perfect love in our lives.

Because herbal baths are sometimes messy and clog drains, many magical practitioners now substitute commercially made herbal soaps. While this seems to be a workable alternative, most readily available herbal soaps have no magical "charge." There are several solutions to this problem. You can infuse the soap with magical properties after its purchase or make your own magical herbal soap if you have the time.

Failing these, you can always whip up a magical soap bag. It is fun, it is easy, it is calming to the nerves, and once you have made one of these beauties, it is doubtful you will ever use a plain washcloth again.

The instructions here are for an herbal soap bag infused with magical success, and the patchwork design used is the Nine Patch. Change the design, colors, and herbal content to suit any other purpose you have in mind.

Materials

- 1 2½" x 7½" strip of purple calico fabric (for magical skill)
- 1 2½" x 7½" strip of yellow calico fabric (for success)
- 1 2½" x 7½" strip of green calico fabric (for luck)
- 1 white washcloth
- cheese grater
- 1 bar soap (a white variety that floats works nicely)
- 2 tablespoons uncooked oatmeal (to soften skin)
- 3 teaspoons cinnamon (for increasing magical skill)
- 3 teaspoons powdered ginger (for success)
- 3 teaspoons allspice (for luck)
- 1 teaspoon salt (for protection)
- 1 yard white ribbon (optional)

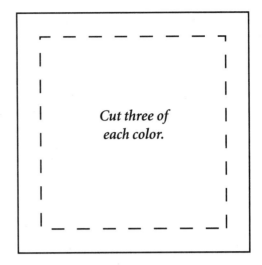

Soap Bag pattern piece.

To Make the Magical Soap Bags

Begin by marking the wrong side of each fabric strip into equal 2½-inch squares according to the pattern piece. Cut out the pieces so you have three squares of each color.

Still working on the wrong side of the fabric squares, mark a ¼-inch seam allowance around each one. Turn the squares over and arrange them in a way that is pleasing to the eye and magically significant to you. In this case, I used the following order:

First row: Purple, yellow, green.

Second row: Green, purple, yellow.

Third row: Yellow, green, purple.

This layout is magically significant as well as attractive. The purple (used to represent an increase in magical skill) flows in one continuous diagonal line so that it is not interrupted by any other color. The green and yellow (used to represent luck and success) each border the purple of the magic as an additional enhancement rather than as a distraction of magical purpose.

With right sides facing, stitch a seam between the first two squares along the seam allowance line. As you stitch, concentrate on the bonding of the two properties symbolized by the colors (in this case, magical skill and success) and chant:

Vibrations meld, vibrations mix—
Into this bit of cloth well fix!
These properties stay bound together
In wind, in rain, or fairest weather!

Add the third square in the same fashion, finishing the first row of squares. Repeat this process for the other two rows, then press open the seams. With right sides facing, pin the first two strips together, making sure to match the seams. Carefully sew the two together. Repeat with the third strip, press open all seams, then press one edge toward the wrong side of the fabric.

Put the finished block face down on the washcloth, pin it securely, and cut around it, adding an extra ¼ inch to the washcloth piece on the side that has the seam allowance pressed under. Sew the patchwork and terrycloth together on three sides, leaving the side with the pressed seam allowance open for filling the bag. Turn the bag right side out.

Filling

Using the cheese grater, grate the bar of soap into a bowl. Add the oatmeal and mix well. Add the cinnamon one teaspoon at a time, and, concentrating on the increasing development of your magical skills, chant with each teaspoon added:

> **Cinnamon, intensify magical skill**
> **And boost the power of my will!**
> **As I will, so be it done—**
> **By Moon and Star and Shining Sun!**

Add the ginger in the same manner as the cinnamon, only this time concentrate on the success of all future magical endeavors. As you add each teaspoon, chant:

> **Ginger, bring your fruitfulness**
> **To my endeavors! Bring success!**
> **As I will, so be it done—**
> **By Moon and Star and Shining Sun!**

Add the allspice and concentrate on its power to add luck to any magical effort. As you add each teaspoon, chant:

> **Allspice, herb of fortune fair!**
> **Your luck with my endeavors share!**
> **As I will, so be it done—**
> **By Moon and Star and Shining Sun!**

Finally, add the salt to protect and seal the herbal vibrations. As you add the salt, chant:

> **Salt, protect and seal this mix!**
> **The powers intermingled, fix!**
> **As I will, so be it done—**
> **By Moon and Star and Shining Sun!**

Mix the ingredients together with your fingers, feeling the cleansing properties of the soap and oatmeal intermingle with the magical properties of the herbs and salt. Concentrate on the purpose of this mixture while saying:

> **Soap will cleanse the body soil!**
> **Herbs will lighten magic toil!**
> **As I will, so be it done—**
> **By Goddess, God, and Ancient Ones!**

Stuff the bag with the mixture, then turn ¼ inch of the terrycloth edge toward the inside and slipstitch the opening shut. Add a ribbon to the top of the bag and hang it from the shower nozzle. This is a great way to keep the soap bag put away when you are not using it for magical baths.

Blue Star of Protection Wallhanging

Project rendered by Georgette Bruhn.

Project design by Dorothy Morrison.

The Wiccan Rede says: "…When misfortune is enow, wear the blue star on thy brow…." That is good advice, but I'm an earthy realist who thinks in preventative terms. I say, "Let the blue star grace thy wall, and misfortune will not fall."

Make this protective pentacle from several shades of blue denim. It is a terrific way to recycle old jeans.

Materials

blue candle

protection incense or lavender flowers

1 yard (approximate yardage) denim scraps

1 yard muslin

sewing thread

¾ yard batting

wide seam binding

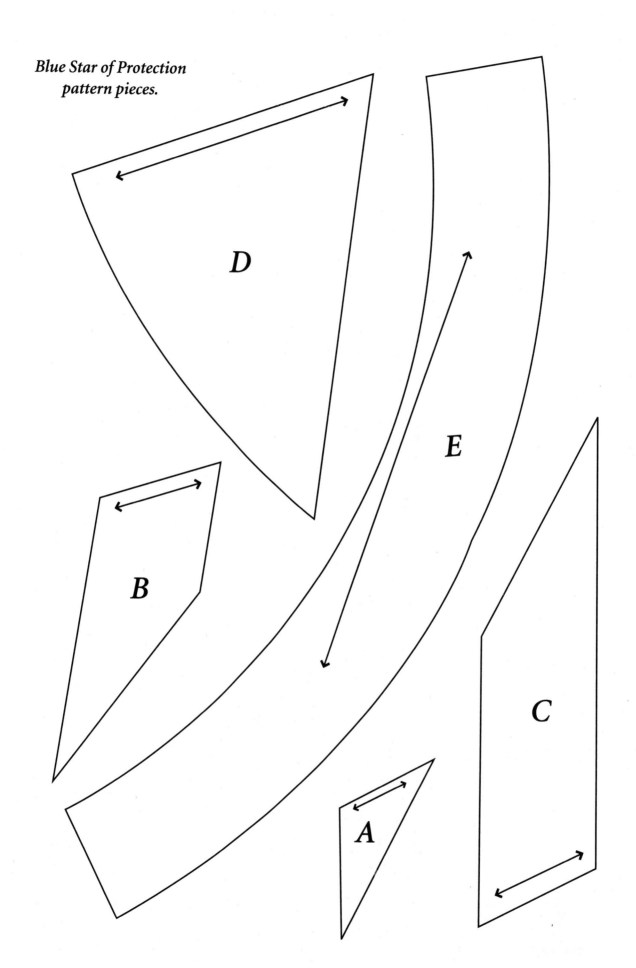

*Blue Star of Protection
pattern pieces.*

To Make the Blue Star of Protection

Light the candle and the incense, then invoke Kali the Destroyer by chanting:

> **Kali, the Destroyer, hear my plea!**
> **Make my home a safe place to be!**
> **Should intruders tread my floor,**
> **Fling them hastily out the door!**

Cut out ten each of pieces A, B, C; five pieces of E from denim; and ten of D from muslin. Lay the pattern on the straight of the grain as marked on each pattern piece. Stitch A, B, C, and D together into ten cones as shown in Figure PQ-7, then stitch two cones to each other so that you have a total of five larger wedges. Sew a piece E to the bottom of each wedge, then stitch the five shapes together to form a pentacle. As you work, chant:

> **I sew the blue star, stitched so well**
> **To hang upon the wall and quell**
> **All misfortune which might fall**
> **Within this home, these rooms or halls!**

Pin the circle to the muslin and batting, then cut around it to form the backing. Quilt by stitching straight lines through the points of the patchwork; there will be five long lines of quilting. As you quilt, chant:

> **Five lines, five paths, four walls and roof!**
> **By Goddess Three! By Horn and Hoof!**
> **By number five, protect this place**
> **And all within this sacred space!**

Seal the edges with seam binding, saying:

> **Oh pentacle of might!**
> **Oh pentacle of power!**
> **I seal your strength within this star,**
> **To grow by passing hour!**

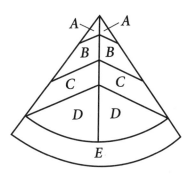

FIGURE PQ-7.

Crazy Quilt Crystal Pouch

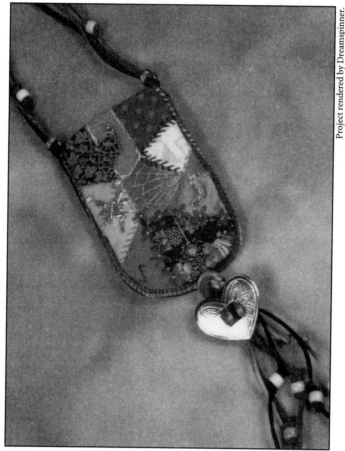

Project design by Dreamspinner of Willowbrook, Illinois.

These crystal pouches are very versatile and can be worn on the hip or around the neck. Make them to hold stones and herbs, related materials for work on a specific chakra, or fill one with tampons, herbal tea, and blessing oil to honor a young woman's first menses.

Materials

fabric scraps

plastic template material (available in arts and crafts stores)

1 6" x 7" piece of muslin for foundation

2 6" x 7" pieces fabric for backing

fusible webbing (such as Heat 'n Bond Lite™)

fabric marking pencil

embroidery needle and flosses

DMC silver metallic embroidery thread

beads and beading needles (optional)

charms, jewelry, et cetera (optional)

2 6" x 7" pieces of silk or other material for lining

2 6" x 7" pieces fleece or felt for batting

strong sewing thread

3 3-yard lengths suede and/or satin cord (for medium hip sling)

silver heart concho

assorted pony beads

small snaps or hook and loop fasteners

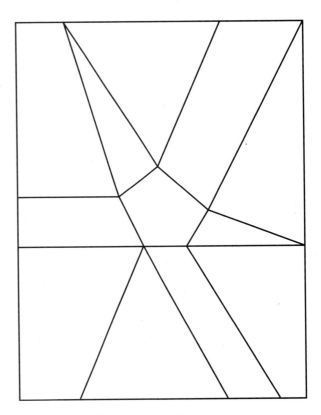

FIGURE PQ-8.

To Make the Crazy Quilt Crystal Pouch

Pre-wash and press all fabrics. Trace the crystal pouch pattern (opposite page) onto template plastic, cut it out, and set it aside. On the paper side of the fusible webbing, trace or draw the medallion shape and cut it out. Then, following the manufacturer's directions, fuse this onto one of your solid fabrics. (If using Heat n' Bond Lite™, fuse it with the iron to the wrong side of the fabric.) When the fused fabric cools, cut the piece out and fuse it to the center of the muslin foundation cloth. (This is the two-step fusing technique.)

Using a pencil and ruler, lightly mark the muslin foundation fabric with straight lines radiating from the center medallion, as shown in Figure PQ-8. Place the template plastic over one of the new shapes, trace, and cut it out. Then flip the template over and trace its shape onto the fusible webbing. Repeat the two-step fusing technique with this shape and another

fabric scrap. (Note: Edges should touch but not overlap. If the edges come up while stitching later, press for a few seconds or stitch in place.)

Continue making templates of each shape, then flipping over and transferring to fusible webbing. Repeat the two-step fusing technique for each fabric until patches cover the foundation cloth. Lay the crystal pouch template over the foundation cloth and move it around until you like what you see through the plastic. Then cut out the pouch top.

Using four strands of embroidery floss, cover the seams with decorative embroidery stitches. Visualize the magic you want to create and choose stitches that are symbolic of that creation. Circular stitches such as the chain, loop, and lazy daisy are representative of the cycle of birth, death, and rebirth or the

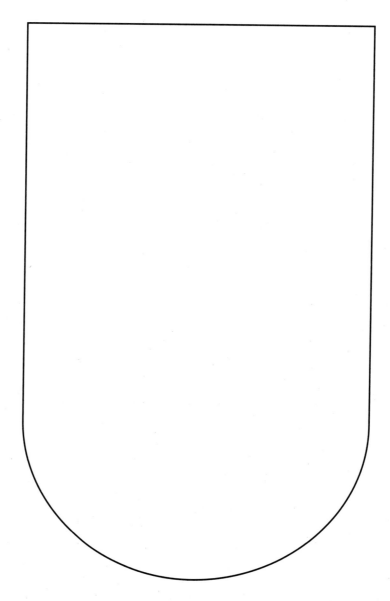

Crystal Pouch pattern.

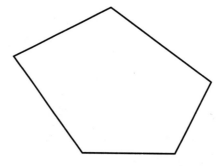

*Pattern piece for
center medallion.*

Wheel of Life (see Chapter Four, "Magical Embroidery," for more information on magical stitches). Honor Grandmother Spider with one strand of silver metallic thread or use straight stitches to form runes. (See diagrams and instructions below. Note: Metallic thread is fragile and breaks easily. Try using a length half as long as you would with regular embroidery floss.)

Embroidering a Spider

To create the spider and web symbol shown in Figure PQ-9, try the following stitches.

WEB. Straight stitches form the web. Stop and begin a new stitch at each spoke.

HEAD. Use two tiny straight stitches and a loop stitch.

BODY. Use a bead.

LEGS. Take a tiny straight stitch, add a bead, then take a longer straight stitch.

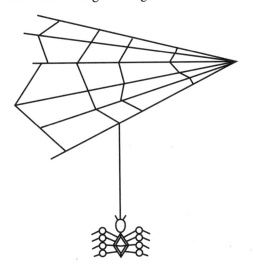

FIGURE PQ-9.

Adding a Rune

For embroidering runes, use four strands of embroidery floss and take straight stitches. Figure PQ-10 is the Channel Rune, which is often used in communication with other realms. Appendix A at the back of the book gives patterns for other runes.

FIGURE PQ-10.

Other Magical Decoration

Attach beads, charms, or jewelry with a sturdy thread. Be careful to position them away from the outer seam allowance.

Lining the Pouch

Using the crystal pouch template as a pattern, cut one from the backing material, two from the fleece or felt, and two from the silk or lining fabric. (Traditionally, crystals are housed in silk, but use your own intuition here.) Lay one of the lining pieces down, right side up. Over this lay the crazy quilt top piece face down.

Lay the fleece or felt on top of this and pin all three layers together. Sew a ¼-inch seam on all sides, leaving 2 inches open for turning. Trim the fleece close to the seam allowance to make turning easier. Turn right side out, stitch the opening closed, and press. Repeat the process for the back of the pouch with the backing material right side up, lining face down, and fleece on top. Seam, turn right side out, stitch the opening, and press. Finally, whipstitch the back to the front.

Making the Laces

Cut the lacing cords in half so you have six pieces that each measure 1½ yards. Hold all six stands together and work from the bottom, sliding them through the heart concho until the heart is about 8 inches from the ends. Knot each strand in back under the concho to prevent slippage, then tie one large knot using all strands just above the concho.

Above this knot, divide the strands into two sets of three. Working from the bottom of the pouch to the top, sew strands on each side using whipstitch, catching a strand here and there to anchor. Randomly knot, bead, and knot again strands at the bottom and sides using pony beads. Sew a few snaps or hook and loop fasteners to the inside for closing. Tie the pouch around your hips or neck and trim the cord strands to the desired length.

Enchanted Notebook or Book of Shadows Cover

Project design by Dorothy Morrison.

Over the years, I've found that keeping my Book of Shadows and magical notes in three-inch loose-leaf binders is much more practical than using traditional stitch-bound books. By sorting through the pages now and then, it is easy to keep the information in order and handy. However, while binders are practical, they look drastically mundane. A quick and easy solution is to cover the book with magical patchwork.

Although any magical patchwork design may be used, the instructions given below are for a log cabin covering, a pattern that suggests perfect balance between light and dark.

Materials

¼   yard each of two dark and two light fabrics

½   yard background fabric

    sewing thread

    3½" square of even-weave cloth

    11½" long piece of even-weave cloth (width determined by width of the loose-leaf binder)

    loose-leaf binder

    paper clip or toothpick

    hot glue

    poster board or lightweight cardboard

To Make the Cover

Use the 3½-inch square of even-weave cloth for the central "building" base. Cut the dark and light fabrics lengthwise into 2-inch strips. Also cut a 2-inch strip from the background fabric.

Ends matching, right sides together, and using a ¼-inch seam allowance, sew a dark strip to one side of the square and trim off the excess. Press out flat. Right sides together and ends matching, sew the same color strip perpendicular to the already joined strip and square. Trim the excess and press out flat.

Working around the square, sew a light strip to the piece so that the strip is perpendicular to the last strip that was joined. (See Figure PQ-11.)

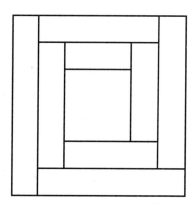

FIGURE PQ-11.

Trim the excess, press out flat, then repeat the process using the same color strip. Repeat the steps with the remaining two fabrics, then stitch a final band of strips from the background material.

Center and Spine

To make the embroidered spine section, cut a piece of even-weave cloth to the exact width and length of the notebook spine.

You can work any design you want for the center square of the cover and use any words on the spine. The center design on the notebook cover in the photo (previous page) is a pentagram design from Karen Everson of Moongate Designs. Consult Appendix A for its cross-stitch pentagram pattern and patterns for the alphabet. (If you aren't familiar with embroidery, see the next chapter and its suggested reading list for assistance.)

Cut two 2½-inch strips as wide as the even-weave from the background fabric. Taking one-inch seams, sew one strip to the top of the even-weave, and the other to the bottom.

Using the front-cover patchwork piece as a pattern, cut a piece from the background cloth. Right sides together and centering the even-weave piece, sew the spine section to the patchwork front. Right sides together and centering the even-weave piece, sew the spine section to the background piece. Trim the top and bottom of the spine section so that it is even with the front and back sections.

Finishing

Lay the piece face down with the open binder on top. Center the seam along the binder spine and tack it in place with a dab of hot glue on each end. Make two tiny cuts in the fabric even with the width of the spine, at both the top and at the bottom. Using a paper clip or toothpick, tuck the flaps under the metal ring base and carefully hot glue the edges in place.

Fold the corner points of the fabric inward and tack them with hot glue. Fold the upper and lower edges over the binder and glue them in place, repeating with the side edges. Cut two pieces of cardboard just a bit smaller than the inside of the binder cover, but large enough to cover the raw edges of the fabric. Hot glue them to the inner front and back.

Enchant your magical book by saying:

Oh book of fiber and design!
Keep information that is mine
Safely tucked between your sides,
For magical notes will here reside!

Place a mulberry leaf inside to protect the contents of the book from outsiders.

Patchwork Tarot Card Bag

Project rendered by Lily Winter.

Project design by Dorothy Morrison.

This pretty patchwork bag is the perfect size for standard-size Tarot cards. Piece it of unbleached muslin, aligning the colors of the Elements with Their proper directions. As you work, concentrate on the insulating and protective powers of the Elements vibrating to keep all negative energies from your deck.

Materials

⅜ yards muslin

small fabric scraps of yellow, red, blue, green, and purple

sewing thread

small hook and loop fasteners

To Make the Tarot Bag

From the muslin, cut two pieces measuring 5 inches by 10 inches for the back and back lining, as well as one piece measuring 5 inches by 6½ inches for the front lining.

Using the pattern pieces on the following page, cut four of piece A, two of piece B, and one each of pieces C and D from the muslin. Then cut one piece A from each of the five colored fabric scraps.

Using ¼-inch seam allowances, piece the bag front together as shown in Figure PQ-12 on page 80. Right sides facing and with bottom edges aligned, sew the front and back together.

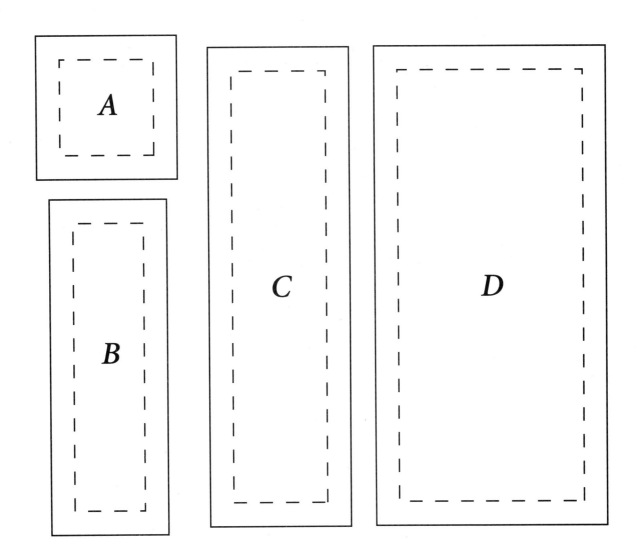

Tarot Card Bag pattern pieces.

		D		
B	A muslin	A green	A muslin	B
	A blue	A purple	A yellow	
	A muslin	A red	A muslin	
		C		

FIGURE PQ-12.

Repeat the process for the lining pieces. Turn the patchwork bag right side out, leaving the lining bag as it is.

With bags back to back, sew the flaps of the patchwork piece and the lining together, seaming all three sides, but leaving the bag front seam open for turning. Turn the bag flap right side out and slip the lining inside the outer bag. Fold ¼ inch under on each front seam, and stitch the seams closed by using either blind stitch or whip stitch. Sew the hook and loop fasteners to the flap area for closing.

Bless the bag using the chant listed for the Crocheted Tarot Bag in the project section for Chapter Five.

Suggested Sources for Quilting Supplies

Norton House
P.O. Box 578
Wilmington, VT 05363
(802) 464-7213

(Send $1 for current catalogue.)

The American Quilter
P.O. Box 7455
Menlo Park, CA 94026
(415) 854-2694

(Send a self-addressed, stamped envelope for brochure and price list.)

The Vermont Patchworks
P.O. Box 229
Shrewsbury, VT 05738
(802) 492-3590

(Send $2 for current catalogue; refundable on first order.)

Suggested Sources for Specialty Fabrics and Trims

Susan of Newport
P.O. Box 3107
Newport Beach, CA 92663
(714) 673-5445

(Send $5 for current catalogue and lace swatches; refundable on first order.)

The Quilt Patch
208 Brigham Street
Marlboro, MA 01752
(508) 480-0194

(Send $1 for current catalogue.)

Quilts and Other Comforts
P.O. Box 394
Wheatridge, CO 80034-0394
(303) 420-4272

(Send $2.50 for current catalogue.)

Suggested Sources for Alternative Patterns

Susan Baxter
Crafts for the Craft from Starwood
9736 North Hassetown Road
Morgantown, IN 46160

Dreamspinner
10 S. 510 Echo Lane #5
Hinsdale, IL 60521-6709

Suggested Reading List

Pauline Campanelli, *The Wheel of the Year: Living the Magical Life* (Llewellyn Publications, St. Paul, Minn., 1988).

Virginia Colton, ed., *Reader's Digest Complete Guide to Needlework* (The Reader's Digest Association, Pleasantville, N.Y., 1979).

Mary Elizabeth Johnson, *Star Quilts* (Clarkson Potter Publishers, New York, N.Y., 1992).

McCall's Big Book of Needlecrafts (ABC Needlework and Crafts Magazines, Inc., 1982). Published in 1989 by Chilton Book Company, Radnor, Penn.; published in 1989 by VNR Publishers, Scarborough,

Judith Montano, *Crazy Quilt Odyssey, Adventures in Victorian Needlework* (C & T Publishing, Lafayette, Calif., 1991).

Magical
Embroidery
Interlacing the Magic

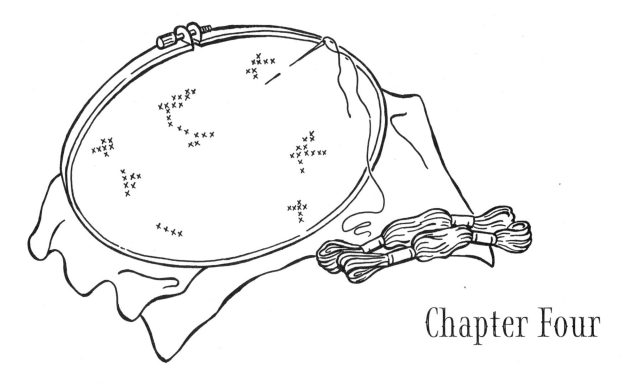

Chapter Four

Embroidery has held a place of importance in nearly every culture, from the delicate work gracing the Oriental kimono to the crisp blue patterns on Dutch linens. A survivor of the ages, embroidery now enhances clothing, household decor, and linens. Because of its versatility, it also lives under glass, in picture frames, and on kitchen walls. Simple or intricate, the result is always an elegant blend of color with an air of magic. But what is the real connection between embroidery and magic?

When I was new to the practice of magic, I learned that the more words in a spell were interlaced with rhyme, the more power the spoken incantation held. The rhyme not only bundled the parts of the spell, but also aided the focus and delivery of concentrated energies. Embroidery, like the rhyme of a spell, intertwines new threads with those already woven in a piece of fabric, gathers them together, and delivers the magical energies into a colorful, new creation.

Modification of a plain piece of fabric by adding stitchwork creates the vibration of a new and different reality. For example, to rid a household of disharmony, stitch a large circle to symbolize the home. Completely cover the inside area with clashing colors and patterns, then satin stitch a heavy black diagonal through the center of the circle to symbolically destroy the conflict and friction. In working this stitchery spell, you exchange your present reality for another of your own creation.

As in any effective spell casting, the purpose, symbology, and colors are important; but with embroidery, the types of stitches and the number of floss strands hold significance, too. Making an outline to list these details will keep you on the right track. It will also boost your magic, for when one commits the intangible to paper, the intangible gains life and forms in reality.

Stitches in Time: Weaving the Rhyme

Through the hand patterns of mind were established, and through the hand they can be reclaimed.

—Myth H

Embroidery is a marvelous instrument for magical expression because the stitches form miniature symbols. Look at embroidery with a fresh eye and seek out stitches that hold personal magic for you. The list below will help you get started.

Chain Stitch

This stitch forms a series of tiny circles that connect in a continuous pattern. It is an excellent choice for working with the cycles of Nature and life. You can also use the chain stitch to symbolize the circle of birth, death, and rebirth.

Satin Stitch

Although this stitch lies flat on the cloth, it forms a spiral by travelling around and around, over and under the cloth, and thus reflects the cone of power. Because the stitch looks much the same on both sides of the fabric, it also may be used to represent Universal balance: "…As above, so below!" Satin stitch is usually used to fill large areas, so it is the perfect stitch for prosperity magic.

Straight Stitch (Backstitch)

Straight stitches symbolize magical pathways. Use two rows of alternating stitches to represent footprints, or a row of zig-zagging stitches to symbolize a winding road. Lengthen stitches to represent great progress. Shorten them to signify caution.

Note: Backstitches—stitches used for outlining—also fall into the straight stitch category.

Blanket Stitch

Some folks hang a horse shoe over their front door to keep their luck from "running out," and the blanket stitch is the lucky horse shoe of the embroidery world. Because this stitch forms tiny lines shooting upward from a straight and solid edge, it works well for binding or sealing magic into any item. Try using it on the hems, cuffs, and necklines of ritual garments; on the edges of altar cloths; and on talismans of luck and protection.

Feather Stitch

This stitch is composed of short lines that alternately zig-zag outward. Magically, it symbolizes pathworking, spiritual connection, and interaction with others. When used to embellish seams, it seals the magic of one piece and connects that magic to the other section.

Lazy Daisy Stitch

Most often used in multiples to create a floral effect, this stitch is a good representation of Nature. Because the stitch forms a circle intersected by a straight stitch, it is also symbolic of the consummated marriage of the Maiden and the Green Man.

Interlaced Running Stitch

In this stitch, a thread of one color winds through a line of running stitches, then the other side intertwines with a thread of complementary hue. Because of the perfect symmetry, it represents the balances of love and hate, light and dark, the right and left hemispheres of the brain, magical energies, and the polarities of male and female. The intertwining threads also symbolize the mingling of ideas and thought.

Plaited Insertion Stitch

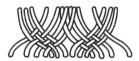

This stitch connects two pieces of fabric, so it is actually a form of weaving, with the fabric acting as the loom and the needle becoming the shuttle. It carries the magic of the needle-crafter's art and serves to connect magical energies, friendships, families, spiritual levels, and so on. The plaited insertion stitch is a spell within itself and its uses are infinite.

Cross Stitch

A depiction of the Solar Cross, the cross stitch is a God symbol. Though this stitch signifies joy, happiness, and success, it represents much more. (See the section "Counted Cross Stitches in a Row Make the Magic Really Grow," next page.) Because two straight stitches of the same length cross each other exactly at midpoint to form the cross stitch, it works well in efforts requiring balance, equality, or justice. The cross stitch is also effective for symbolizing the symmetrical duality of the Lord and Lady.

Herringbone Stitch

A version of the cross stitch, the herringbone stitch differs in that the cross does not form at midpoint, but at the top third of the first stitch and the bottom third of the second. Use it when working with relationships or unions of any kind, from romantic to business.

Interlaced Maltese Cross Stitch

Because this stitch forms a very ornate equal-armed cross, I use it to symbolize the four seasons or the power of the Elements. A thread of separate color intertwines through the base stitches to form this design, which is perfect for the connection of Akasha to the other Elements, or for the force that changes the seasons.

Smyrna Stitch

Another variation of the cross stitch, this beauty is sometimes known as the double cross stitch. It forms a good depiction of the eight Sabbats in the Wheel of the Year.

Counted Cross Stitches in a Row Make the Magic Really Grow

The resurgence of the art of counted cross stitch within the Pagan community gave me pause for thought. Was it the sudden availability of new subject matter? The rhythm of the stitching? The idea of taking a blank piece of fabric and transforming it into a new creation? Did the stitch, itself, hold the magic? The answer to every question is, "Yes!" In the *Elder Futhark Workbook*, Myth H explains:

> Counted cross stitching is not worked from a pre-transferred design. Instead, the pattern is embroidered onto blank fabric— usually an even-weave—by reference to an auxiliary chart. You simply count the number of stitches on the pattern and then embroider that number, in position, onto the material.

> There are two basic ways you can make the stitches—one at a time, or sequentially (in rows). Visually, they appear to be identical…but magically they behave differently. Magically, sequentially formed stitches indicate a continuous stream of force. One-at-a-time stitches show continuous, but interlocking movement.

According to Myth H, the underlying leg represents need, which invokes the forces of magic. The leg crossing over the top reflects action, or the response to initiated magic.

A major consideration when working with cross stitches is the "flow" of the stitch, because it affects the magic. For instance, if the underlying leg runs bottom to top, the need flows upward. Completing the stitch with a top to bottom overlying leg causes the responsive energy or anticipated action to flow downward. These techniques work well in efforts of creation, banishment, and balance.

If your intention is to honor, try stitching both legs in the same direction. For example, stitchery worked to glorify the Lady is most magically effective when both legs travel upward. The opposite is true of projects honoring the Dark Lord.

The direction in which you stitch individual rows also affects the magical result. For goals in which increase or creation are necessary—prosperity, love, or good health—rows that run left to right work well. If decrease is the key note in your magical working—dieting, breaking bad habits, or peaceful separation—the magic flows more easily if the rows of stitching run right to left.

Magical Results Received Depend Upon the Proper Weave

For successful magical embroidery, choosing the proper fabric type is imperative. There are two categories of embroidery fabric: even-weave and common-weave. Not only do the physical properties of these fabric types differ greatly, but also their magical energies vibrate to opposite ends.

Even-Weave Fabric

Even-weave fabric has the same number of warp and weft threads in each square inch. It contains both physical and magical balance, and vibrates toward order, unity, and perfect harmony. Most even-weave fabrics have the look of tiny checkerboards, making them an excellent choice for counted cross stitch. The three most common types of fabric in this category are Aida cloth, Hardanger, and single thread even-weave. Both Aida and Hardanger have easily discernable checkerboard patterns, making embroidery graphs easy to follow. Single thread cloth has no pattern, and while it is my personal favorite for working traditional stitches, it is more difficult to use than the other two even-weaves.

Common-Weave Fabrics

Most fabrics fall into the common-weave category. Common-weave materials have an unequal number of threads per square inch, so instead of reflecting balance and order, they mirror chaotic motion. This magically versatile cloth can be used to change unsuitable circumstances. A design of organized beauty may be embroidered on the common-weave, bringing harmony and order to the unequivalent thread count reflected in the cloth. The lover of counted cross stitch can also use common-weave by attaching waste canvas, working the stitches, then removing the canvas thread by thread.

How Many Strands Can Be Threaded Through the Eye of a Needle?

The number of strands of thread, yarn, or floss used in stitches provides magic of its own, and can work wonders for any magical stitchery project. Here are some numerological basics that are easy to remember.

ONE. This is the number of self, the ego, and the personality. In embroidery, backstitching is generally done with one strand of floss. Though it is important to put oneself (or the person for whom you are working the project) into the "finished picture," too much self can backfire disastrously and cause ego problems, arrogance, and pomposity. If you feel that outlining alone doesn't put enough self into the project, interlace a single strand here and there for proper balance.

TWO. This number symbolizes balance and is the number of strands most commonly used in ordinary embroidery projects. Try using a lighter and a darker shade of the same color together. This gives a rich effect to your work and is truly magical in Universal symmetry, balancing the light and dark opposites of every situation in the cosmos. The number two is also representative of the duality of the Lord and Lady and the wisdom of the High Priestess of the Tarot.

THREE. "…Ever mind the rule of three…." This number relates to the laws of karma, which maintain that each act or deed—good or bad—is returned three times over to its sender. Use this number when invoking or easing life's lessons, or when working with the God and Goddess in Their triple forms.

FOUR. Four strands work well in projects dealing with the change of the seasons and the topographical directions of East, South, West, and North. Also the number of solidity and support, use it in projects worked to add stability.

FIVE. The Elements—Air, Fire, Water, Earth, and Spirit—equal the number five. This number also works well for projects dealing with money, travel, and adventure.

Six. Use six strands in matters of love and harmony, or for projects pertaining to home, family, and related responsibilities.

Feel free to use as many strands as you find suitable for the stitches in your project. I usually don't use more than six, because it is difficult to work neat stitches or even thread a needle with a greater number.

Enchanting Knots and Stitches

Before beginning any type of magical embroidery project, bless your materials, for by their incorporation, they become magical tools. The ritual can be simple or complex. The main objective is to make the ceremony personally meaningful; you are the magician and the magic stems from your imagination. (If you need ideas or help, see the first chapter of this book.)

When you begin the project, set the spell into motion by enchanting the first stitch. Use the chant below or construct one of your own.

> **Oh piercing needle, that which gleams**
> **[Your intention] is the reason for this spell**
> **Stitch its purpose through this weave**
> **And bind it thoroughly and well.**

Of course, no enchantment would be complete without a binding to hold the magic. One way is to fix each portion when you finish with a strand of floss. As you tie the knot, chant something such as:

> **I bind this portion of my spell**
> **With steel and fiber tied so tight!**
> **Hold these handmade stitches well!**
> **Contain their magic and their might!**

Another binding method is to work each thread end into the others four times and chant:

> **Maiden, Mother, Horned One, Crone:**
> **Let this work be bound with patience**
> **and love!**

Embroidery is a very versatile form of magic and with a little imagination, even the most mundane patterns can become real works of enchantment. Don't be afraid to vary from a design by choosing a different stitch, another color, or a different method or material. Potent magic often relies upon a last minute change here or there. Remember that magical embroidery doesn't always have to look like the mundane type. It is perfectly acceptable to fill a project with all types of stitches, combining the light and dainty with the rich and heavy. Unlike mundane embroidery, you will find each magical project has a life of its own—a uniqueness in color, symbology, and content. Remember to have fun and let your imagination run wild, for imagination, itself, is the truest form of magic.

Some basic knowledge of embroidery stitches is necessary to complete the projects in this chapter. If you have never embroidered before, or some of the project stitches are not familiar to you, try one of the books in this chapter's suggested reading list. You could also pick up a needlecraft magazine at your local newstand or supermarket. Nearly all of them have a general instructions section that contains this information.

Loving Dream Pillow

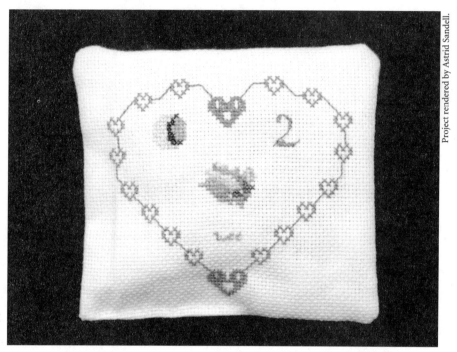

Project design by Brenda Moslener of "A Needle Bewitched."

Although dream pillows are used for no other reason than to ensure restful sleep and pleasant dreams, many dream pillows also have additional specific intentions. Sometimes the dreamer wishes for prophetic dreams about love, a new house, a child not yet born, or a picture of the future. Sometimes the dreamer seeks help in finding a lost item, in aiding the memory, or in bringing insight. Whatever your intention, allow it to guide the creation of your dream pillow.

Make this dream pillow to enhance dreams about love. Most of the symbols found in this design are common images of love and need no explanation. The crescent moon symbolizes the Goddess, magic, and feminine energies, which charge the dream pillow. The glyphs at the bottom of the heart are ancient talismanic symbols of love from the Hebrew Book of Raziel, a copy of which is in the British Museum. The number two is included because it is the number of duality and relationships.

Magical Embroidery: Interlacing the Magic

Materials

2 6" squares of white even-weave cloth (14-count or 16-count Aida is recommended)

embroidery floss (the legend is made of DMC colors)

tapestry and sewing needles

sewing thread

fiberfill

glass seed beads (optional)

rose petals

lavender flowers

1 daisy

small piece of rose quartz

To Make the Loving Dream Pillow

The Loving Dream Pillow pattern and its legend appear on the next page. The pattern includes a waxing Moon, while the photo on the opposite page shows a waning Moon. You can use whichever one suits your purpose.

Centering the design, cross stitch it on one piece of fabric. While you embroider, visualize the person you love or concentrate on the love you seek. Place the right sides together, and stitch around the pillow leaving a 2-inch opening in one side.

Turn the pillow casing inside out. Gently insert two thin layers of fiberfill into the pillow. Fill the center between the fiberfill layers with the rose petals, lavender, the daisy, and rose quartz. Stitch the opening closed.

Before use, charge your dream pillow in moonlight or starlight, or perform a dedication ritual if you like. Before sleep, bathe in warm, rose-scented water, and meditate upon what your heart wants most. Place the dream pillow beneath your bed pillow and sleep.

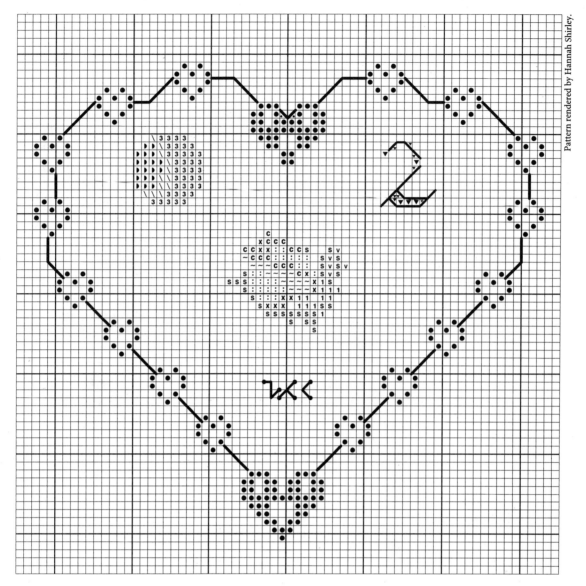

Loving Dream Pillow pattern.

Loving Dream Pillow Legend (DMC Colors)

Stitch	DMC #	Color			
❱	318	Steel Gray LT	:	3712	Salmon MD
\	319	Pistachio Green VY DK	c	3713	Salmon VY LT
▼	320	Pistachio Green MD	x	3328	Salmon DK
1	367	Pistachio Green DK			
S	368	Pistachio Green LT	3 }	DMC #762	Pearl Gray VY LT
v	369	Pistachio Green VY LT		Balger Silver	Silver
~	761	Salmon LT			
●	793	Cornflower Blue MD			

French knots and glyph below the rose are DMC #794 (Cornflower Blue LT). Glass seed beads may be substituted for French knots.

A Witch's "Blessed Be" Sampler

Project rendered by Becca Allen.

Project design based on a pattern from InaRae Ussack of Craft/Crafts Magazine.

Stitch the Witch's "Blessed Be" Sampler to protect your home or your ritual room. It is also a wonderful reminder that everything within our realm is blessed, sacred, and deserving of respect.

Use two strands of floss for the stitch work. Feel free to substitute the colors you feel best suit your needs. Do the outlines with one strand using backstitch—around the cauldron and fireplace with black, and around the crystal ball with 931 or a brighter blue. **Note:** The shadows are not outlined.

Materials

piece of common-weave or even-weave fabric at leas 161 squares high by 200 squares wide

embroidery floss (the legend is made of DMC colors)

To Make the Blessed Be Sampler

The pattern for the "Blessed Be" sampler is shown on the following two pages. Its legend appears on page 96.

Witch's "Blessed Be" Sampler Legend (DMC Colors)

Stitch	DMC #	Color	Stitch	DMC #	Color
X	310	Black	8	3821	Straw MD
b	1	White	?	3820	Straw DK
+	762	Pearl Gray VY LT	5	743	Yellow MD
(	415	Pearl Gray	–	3046	Yellow Beige MD
=	318	Steel Gray LT	1	3045	Yellow Beige DK
▼	414	Steel Gray DK	c	727	Topaz VY LT
&	413	Pewter Gray DK	r	726	Topaz LT
✓	971	Pumpkin	9	725	Topaz
o	721	Orange Spice MD	••	333	Blue Violet VY DK
^	720	Orange Spice DK	/	791	Cornflower Blue VY DK
:	817	Coral Red VY DK	<	3816	Celadon Green MD
♡	436	Tan	e	3815	Celadon Green DK
!	434	Brown LT	B	815	Garnet MD
s	433	Brown MD	∅	988	Forest Green MD
~	898	Coffee Brown VY DK	#	500	Blue Green VY DK
d	938	Coffee Brown ULT DK	m	816	Garnet
△	3822	Straw LT	ɪ	561	Jade VY DK

Stitch the sampler according to the pattern and legend. When finished, sprinkle the back with water and press it with a hot iron. Consecrate the piece to protect you by chanting:

**Oh little sampler of many stitches,
Protect me from what ill may fall!**

**Keep evil far from nooks and niches!
Keep safe each closet, room, and hall!
Protect my family and all of those
Who enter here in friendship's love!
Keep them safe and heal their woes!
Bring joy and happiness from above!**

Celtic Knotwork Embroidered Bookmark

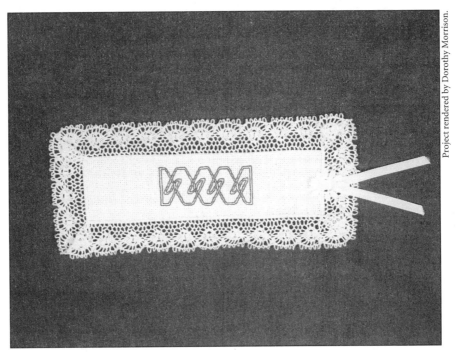

Project rendered by Dorothy Morrison.

Project design by Miss Chiff of Misc. by Miss Chiff.

This design is a modification of the Celtic knotwork representation of the hazel tree by A. B. Firethorn Designs. As the hazel tree is significant of wisdom, make this bookmark for a student or for anyone wishing to retain knowledge.

Materials

2" x 4" piece of 18-count Aida cloth

13 inches ⅛" satin ribbon

embroidery floss (color of your choice)

13 inches ½" cotton lace edging

To Make the Bookmark

Beginning on the third row of the fabric, sew the lace around the edges. Sew the ribbon on top of the inner edge of the lace, securing it well. This not only keeps the edges from fraying, but also seals the edges from picking up negative energy.

Stitch the design according to the pattern on the following page. Use a backstitch and work from the center outward.

Wash the bookmark in cool, soapy water. Rinse well, then blot with a towel to remove the excess water. Place the bookmark face down on the towel and press dry with a hot

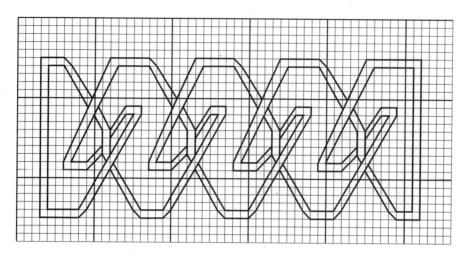

Celtic Knotwork Bookmark pattern.

iron, then consecrate it to the hazel tree and the Crone, saying:

> Oh, Crone of knowledge, hear my plea!
> Grant the wisdom of the hazel tree!

Unravel the Mysteries and strengthen the brain
So that all that I read shall be retained!

Triple Goddess Moon Phase Sampler

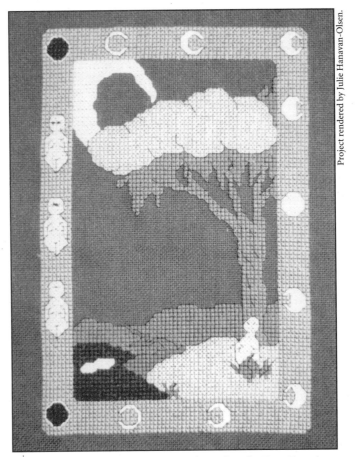

Project rendered by Julie Hanavan-Olsen.

Project design by Julie Hanavan-Olsen of Urtha Lun Creations.

This delightful sampler celebrates the Triple Goddess, the phases of the Moon, and the joys of our planet. Make it to infuse your magical working space with Goddess energy.

Materials

a piece of even-weave fabric at least 130 squares high by 100 squares wide

embroidery floss (the legend is made of DMC colors)

To Make the Sampler

The pattern for the Triple Goddess Moon Phase Sampler is on the following page. Its legend appears on page 101.

Cross stitch the sampler according to the pattern and legend.

Pattern rendered by Hannah Shirley.

Triple Goddess Moon Phase Sampler pattern.

Triple Goddess Moon Phase Sampler Legend (DMC Colors)

Stitch	DMC #	Color		Stitch	DMC #	Color
□	1	White		x	898	Coffee Brown VY DK
>	310	Black		–	934	Black Avocado Green
U	319	Pistachio Green VY DK		(	3753	Antique Blue ULT VY LT
\	320	Pistachio Green MD				
◊	400	Mahogany DK		**Half Stitches**		
~	410	Steel Gray DK		•	336	Navy Blue
1	644	Beige Gray MD		**Outline Stitches**		
					310	Black

Consecrate the finished sampler to the Goddess energies of the Moon by chanting:

**Rising Crescent, shining bright
Bring the Maiden's joy to me each night!
Fullest Moon so high above**

**Bring the Mother's peace and love!
Waning crescent, sharply honed
Bring the ancient wisdom of the Crone!
And Moon of darkness, Moon so new
Give me strength to start anew!**

Pentagram Coffee Mug

Project design by Alodi of Field-N-Forest.

Project rendered by Dorothy Morrison.

This project is inexpensive to make and takes very little time. Although most people would use the mug for coffee, tea, or other beverages, it also makes a terrific holder for writing tools, candles, or other small magical objects. Personalize the mug by changing the color scheme or the "an it harm none" heading. Use your imagination. Stitch your magical name in the "Modified Theban Alphabet" shown in Appendix A or add a row of symbolic runes.

Materials

1 cross stitch mug

embroidery floss

Pentagram Coffee Mug Legend (DMC Colors)

Stitch	DMC #	Color
3	310	Black
●	312	Navy Blue LT
✗	995	Electric Blue DK

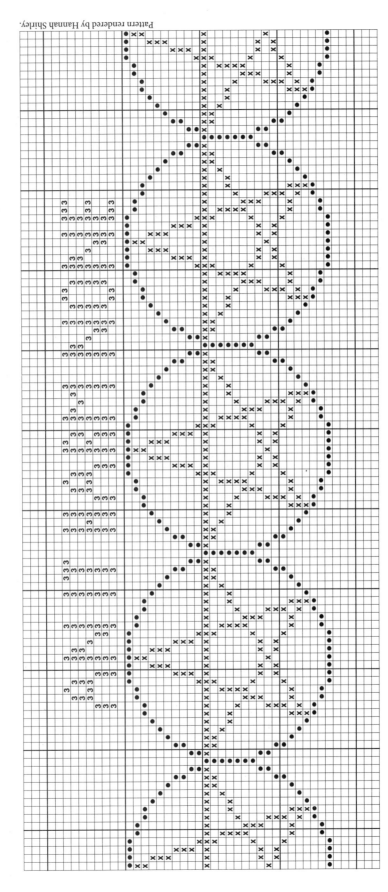

Pentagram Coffee Mug pattern.

Runic Pin or Pendant

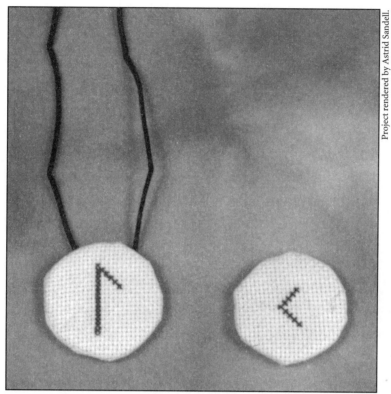

Project rendered by Astrid Sandell.

Project design by Myth H of Myth H Designs.

Tell the Universe what changes you would like to see in your life by wearing this runic pendant or lapel pin. This project makes use of the runic designs found in the *Elder Futhark Runes Counted Cross Stitch Patterns & Workbook* from the Myth H Magical Needlework Series. These are so simple and inexpensive to make that you can construct several at one sitting.

Materials

18-count even weave fabric at least 30 squares by 30 squares

embroidery floss
(color of your choice)

lightweight plastic (an old plastic cup will do)

compass (for drafting circles)

sewing thread and needle

hot glue

small scrap of felt

jewelry pin (available at arts-and-crafts stores, K-Mart, or Wal-Mart; optional)

1   yard satin or suede cording (optional)

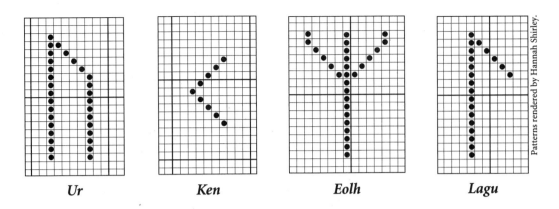

| Ur | Ken | Eolh | Lagu |

Runic Pin/Pendant patterns.

To Make the Runic Pin/Pendant

Shown here are the patterns for Ur (strength, growth, transformation, and passage), which is great for students; Ken (creation, the inner voice, arts and crafts), the rune best suited to those led by the Muses; Eolh (protection, courage, and endurance), which repels negative forces; and Lagu (intuition, extended awareness, and altered states), for those who wish to give their magical abilities a real boost. You will find more rune patterns in Appendix A in the back of the book.

Beginning in the center of the fabric, cross stitch the rune of your choice. As you stitch, chant and concentrate on the purpose of your project. For instance, if you are working with the rune of Lagu you might wish to chant something like:

Rune of Lagu! Rune of intuition!
Bring extended awareness! It's my ambition!
Increase my psychism and magical power
By second and minute, by quarter and hour!

With the compass and a pencil, draw a very light circle around the stitched rune. Then draw the same size circle on the felt, and a circle ¼ inch smaller on the plastic. Cut out the circles with the scissors. With a needle and thread, make long running stitches all around the circle line on the even weave but do not tie a knot. Lay the embroidered piece face down and center the plastic circle on top. Tightly draw up the thread end to gather the basting stitches around the piece of plastic. Knot well and trim any excess fabric from the back.

To make the pendant, cut the cords in half and hot glue one piece to each side of the plastic circle. Hot glue the felt piece on top. Tie the cords to suitable length and trim the excess.

If the lapel pin is more to your liking, hot glue the jewelry pin to the back of the felt or secure it with stitches.

Consecrate the finished pendant or pin to the deity of your choice or to Odin, the Bringer of the Runes.

"I Am the Goddess Who Cradles the Earth"

Project design by Julie Hanavan-Olsen of Urtha Lun Creations.

This is a beautiful depiction of the Goddess holding the Earth clasped in her arms—nurturing, loving, and protecting all of its inhabitants. Julie's original graph was a single Goddess beneath a crescent moon; however, I have modified the graph a bit so that the motif repeats itself to depict all of the Lady's children. I suggest joining five Goddesses together and stitching them with different colors of skin tone and hair to represent Caucasian, African, Asian, Latin, and Native American, for the Goddess lives within each of us.

Materials

even-weave fabric at least 55 squares by 100 squares for each Goddess stitched

embroidery floss (color of your choice)

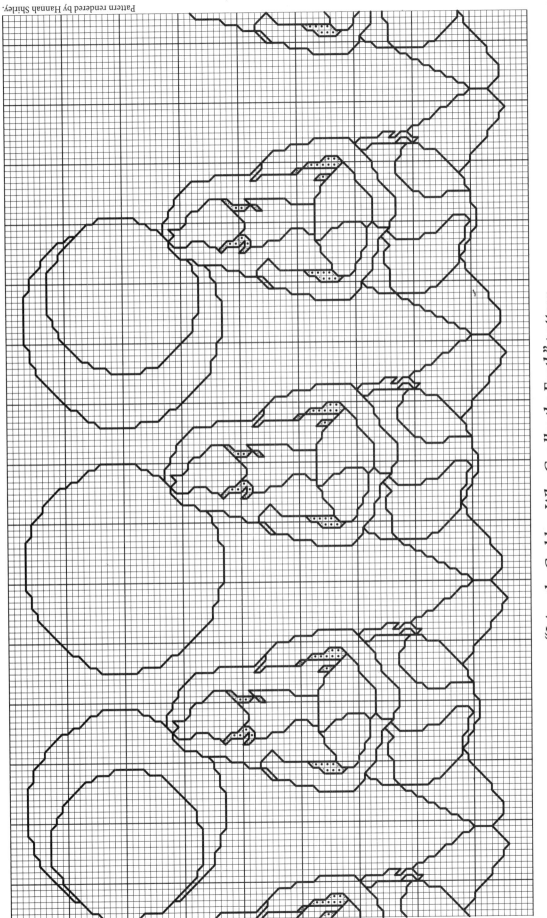

"I Am the Goddess Who Cradles the Earth" pattern.

To Make the Sampler

Because of the variety of skin tones and hair coloring possibilities, no legend is included for this project. However, hair shading is marked for your convenience.

Personalize the Earth Mother and stitch Her in shades that are meaningful to you. Using the following chant is a wonderful way to empower the Goddess sampler:

I am the Goddess Who cradles the Earth!

I am the Goddess Who gave the World birth!

I am the Goddess Who conceived the Young Child!

I am the Goddess Who is young, free, and wild!

I am the Goddess Who is older than Age!

I am the Goddess Who turns life's every page!

I am each creature—tremendous and small!

I am the Goddess! I am many and all!

Suggested Sources for Specialty Threads and Supplies

Craft Gallery
P.O. Box 145
Swampscott, MA 01907
(508) 744-2334
(Send $2 for current catalogue.)

Herrschners, Inc.
Hoover Road
Stevens Point, WI 54481
(715) 341-4554
(Free catalogue.)

Joan Toggitt
35 Fairfield Place
West Caldwell, NJ 07006
(201) 575-5410
(Write or call for price list.)

LACIS
2982 Adeline Street
Berkeley, CA 94703
(415) 843-7178
(Send $1 for current catalogue.)

Main Stitches
Attention: Carolyn Rogers
526A South Main Street
Sikeston, MO 63801
(314) 471-5658
(Write or call for prices.)

Things Japanese
9805 N.E. 116th Street
Suite 7160
Kirkland, WA 98034
(206) 821-2287
(Send $2 for current catalogue.)

Suggested Sources for Patterns, Stitches, and Ideas

Susan Baxter
Crafts for the Craft from Starwood
9736 N. Hassetown Road
Morgantown, IN 46160

Miss Chiff
Misc. by Miss Chiff
10131 East 32nd St., Apt. C
Tulsa, OK 74146-1405

Alodi
Field-N-Forest
512 N. Douglas Boulevard
Midwest City, OK 73130

Julie Hanavan-Olsen
Urtha Lun Creations
4855 West Hillside Dr.
Eugene, OR 97405

Myth H
6920 Ashburn
Houston, TX 77061

Brenda Moslener
A Needle Bewitched
23511 Aliso Creek Road #120
Aliso Viejo, CA 92626
(Please send $1 for catalog of items.)

InaRae Ussack
Craft/Crafts Magazine
P.O. Box 441
Ponderay, ID 83852

Karen Everson
Moongate Designs
44791 Windmill Dr.
Canton, MI 48187

Suggested Reading List

Pauline Campanelli, *The Wheel of the Year: Living the Magical Life* (Llewellyn Publications, St. Paul, Minn., 1988).

Virginia Colton, ed., *Reader's Digest Complete Guide to Needlework* (The Reader's Digest Association, Pleasantville, N.Y., 1979).

Judith Montano, *Crazy Quilt Odyssey: Adventures in Victorian Needlework* (C & T Publishing, Lafayette, Calif., 1991).

McCall's Big Book of Needlecrafts (ABC Needlework and Crafts Magazines, Inc., 1982). Published in 1989 by Chilton Book Company, Radnor, Penn.; published in 1989 by VNR Publishers, Scarborough, Ontario, Canada.

Mildred Graves Ryan, *The Complete Encyclopedia of Stitchery* (Doubleday & Company, Inc., Garden City, N.Y., 1979).

Magical
Crochet
Chaining the Magic

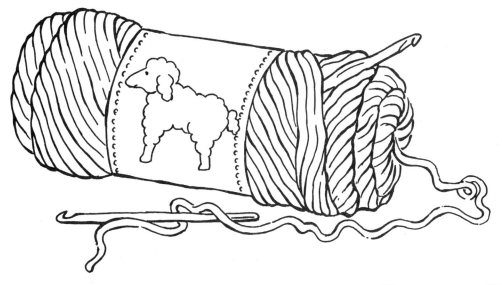

Chapter Five

Ram Dass, the well-known spiritual teacher, tells a delightful story about one of his lectures that took place in the early seventies. It was the era of the flower children and his audience usually ranged in age from fifteen to twenty-five. One night, a little old lady meandered down the center aisle and seated herself in the front row. She looked so out of place in her saddle oxfords, netted hair, and fruit-laden hat, Dass couldn't help but notice her.

When he spoke about his inner journey, discussed the wonders of psychedelic drugs and the magic of altered consciousness, the old woman nodded knowingly. No matter how extreme or explicit his stories became, she still nodded as if to say she knew exactly how he felt. Intrigued with the little old lady and her attitude, he finally beckoned her up to the podium.

"Oh, thank you so much!" A smile overtook her wrinkled face. "That's just the way I understand things to be."

"How do you know?" he asked. "I don't believe you've ever taken a psychedelic drug in your life. What have you done in your life that allows you to know these things?"

At that, she leaned over conspiratorially, winked at him and whispered, "I crochet!"

The Magical Basics of Crochet

Crochet is formed by connecting a series of loops or chains that symbolize the Circle and the cycle of birth, death, rebirth with every stitch. If that's not magic enough, the patterns and symbols that take shape during the process hold their own enchantment.

There are three basic types of crochet: simple stitches, motifs, and filet. Each of these types vibrates toward different areas.

Simple stitches represent balance and stability. They also mirror emotion and feeling, making them an excellent focal point for spellworking.

Motifs have a distinctly different feel and they fall into two categories: two-dimensional shapes and granny squares. Two-dimensional shapes form actual symbols—hearts, clover, flowers, et cetera—and are most often sewn together to complete a particular picture or idea. They have a direct and straightforward energy that vibrates toward the shape of the symbol created.

The granny square motif may take on several shapes and forms: circular, octagonal, hexagonal, and rectangular. Standard "grannies" are worked in clusters of three stitches, making them sacred to the Goddess. These motifs share the energies of both simple stitches and two-dimensional shapes.

Filet crochet is a solid shape in a lacy mesh background. Unlike motifs, filet is crocheted in a solid piece and has a very fluid energy current. The stability of the solid shape contrasts with the mesh's firm but delicate appeal to the cosmos. Filet also acts as a magical netting that keeps good vibrations in and locks out the bad. Patterns graphed specifically for counted cross stitch may also be crocheted, provided that the designs consist only of whole stitches and contain no color changes.

Stitches that hold magical vibration for me and the directions for working them are listed on the following pages.

Stitch Abbreviations

The following abbreviations are used throughout the instructions for the following magical stitches and in the instructions for the magical crochet projects in this chapter.

Chain (ch), slip stitch (slst), single crochet (sc), half-double crochet (hdc), double crochet (dc), treble crochet (trc), double treble (dtr), stitch (st), begin (beg), repeat (rpt), space (sp), skip (sk), block (bl), yarn over (yo).

Magical Crochet Stitches

Woven Stitch

This stitch makes a sturdy and heavy piece of cloth. Use it for projects involving relationships or where strength and unity are important. This is also a good stitch to use when you feel the need to tightly interweave a new asset or character trait into your personality.

Work the woven stitch on a multiple of three chains plus three and crochet as follows:

Row 1. Sk 2 ch, 1 sc, *ch 1, sk 1 ch, 1 sc*, ch 2, turn.

Row 2. *1 sc in ch sp of previous row, ch1*, 1 sc in the turning ch sp, ch 2, turn. Repeat from Row 2.

Diagonal Stitch

The diagonal stitch is an excellent choice for getting rid of something in your life, such as bad habits, fair weather friends, or negative energy. A double diagonal line forms over each cluster pattern and stamps out the problem.

Work the diagonal stitch on a multiple of four chains plus one and crochet as follows:

Row 1. Sk 1 ch, *1 sc in each ch*, ch 2, turn.

Row 2. *Sk 1 st, dc in each of next 3 sts, insert hook in last skipped stitch, yo, draw through an elongated loop, yo, draw through 2 loops*, 1 dc in last st, ch 1, turn.

Row 3. Sk 1 st, *1 sc in each st*, 1 sc in turning ch, ch 2, turn. Repeat from Row 2.

Ripple Stitch

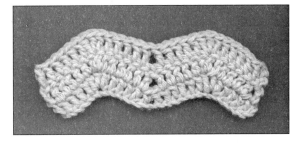

The ripple stitch symbolizes waves, making it sacred to the Goddess and Water deities. It is also a good stitch to use when working projects to soften life's little "ups and downs."

Work the ripple stitch on a multiple of thirteen chains and crochet as follows:

Row 1. Sk 3 ch, dc in the next 4 ch, 3 dc in the next ch, dc in the next 5 ch, *sk 2 ch, dc in the next 5 ch, 3 dc in the next ch, dc in the next 5 ch*, ch 3, turn.

Row 2. Sk 1 st, dc in each st up to the center st of the 3-dc cluster, 3 dc in the center st, dc in the next 5 sts, *sk 2 sts, dc in the next 5 sts, 3 dc in the next st, dc in the next 5 sts*, end with 4 dc, sk 1 dc, 1 dc in turning ch, ch 3, turn. Repeat from Row 2.

Basket Weave Stitch

This stitch is absolutely fabulous for creating balance in one's life. Change the colors intermittently to represent the chakras for healing, the Elements for emotional health, or any quality you find lacking. Gifts made with this stitch are extremely magical.

Work the basket weave stitch on a multiple of six chains and crochet as follows:

Row 1. Sk 3 ch, *1 dc in the next ch*, ch 2, turn.

Rows 2 and 3. Sk 1 dc, *(1 post around the front; i.e. yo, insert hook back to front between the next two sts, then back again between the st being worked and the one after it—complete the dc. One front post dc made) 3 times, (1 post dc around the back; i.e., same as working the front post

except that stitch is begun by yo, and inserting the hook from front to back 3 times*, (1 front post dc) 3 times, 1 dc in top of turning ch, ch 2, turn.

Rows 4 and 5. Sk 1 dc, *(1 back post dc) 3 times, (1 front post dc) 3 times*, (1 back post dc) 3 times, 1 dc in top of turning ch, ch 2, turn. Repeat from Row 2.

Arcade Stitch

Because of its five-stitch shell pattern, you can use the arcade stitch to represent the balance of the Elements. As this stitch forms a triangle beneath each shell, it is also the ideal pattern to use for invoking the Lady's power and grace.

Work the arcade stitch on a multiple of six chains plus eight and crochet as follows:

Row 1. Sk 1 ch, 1 sc in each of the next 2 ch, *ch 3, sk 3 ch, 1 sc in each of the next 3 ch*, ch 3, sk 3 ch, 1 sc in each of the last 2 ch, ch 1, turn.

Row 2. 1 sc in 2nd sc, *5 dc in ch-3 sp, 1 sc in 2nd sc of 3-sc group*, turn.

Row 3. *ch 3, 1 sc in each of 3 center dc*, ch 2, 1 sc in turning ch, ch 3, turn.

Row 4. 2 dc in ch-2 sp, *1 sc in 2nd sc, 5 dc in ch-3 sp*, 1 sc in 2nd sc, 3 dc in ch-3 sp, ch 1, turn.

Row 5. 1 sc in each of the first 2 dc, *ch 3, 1 sc in each of the 3 center dc*, ch 3, 1 sc in the last dc, 1 sc in the turning ch, ch 1, turn. Repeat from Row 2.

Starburst Stitch

The starburst stitch may be used to represent the God, the power of the Sun, and the deities of Fire. Use it, too, in efforts to promote joy, happiness, and success.

Work the starburst stitch on a multiple of eight chains plus ten and crochet as follows:

Row 1. Sk 1 ch, 1 sc *sk 3 ch, 9 dc in next ch, sk 3 ch, 1 sc*, ch 3, turn.

Row 2. Sk 1 sc, 4-dc cluster over the next 4 sts [(yo, insert hook, draw up a loop, yo, draw through 2 loops) in each st, yo, draw through 5 loops)], *ch 4, 1 sc, ch 3, 9-dc cluster over the next 9 sts*, ch 4, 1 sc, ch 3, 5-dc cluster, ch 4, turn.

Row 3. 4 dc in the top of 5-dc cluster, 1 sc in the sc, *9 dc in the top of 9-dc cluster, 1 sc in the sc*, 5 dc in the top of the 4-dc cluster, ch 3, turn.

Row 4. Sk 1 dc, *9-dc cluster, ch 4, 1 sc, ch 3*, 1 sc in turning ch, ch 1, turn.

Row 5. 1 sc, *9 dc in the top of the 9-dc cluster, 1 sc*, 1 sc in the turning ch, ch 3, turn. Repeat from Row 2.

Brick Stitch

Use this stitch to invoke the solidity of the Earth deities. Because the "bricks" run in different directions, it is a very active stitch and also works well in efforts to increase physical energy, vigor, and stamina.

Work the brick stitch on a multiple of four chains plus six and crochet as follows:

Row 1. Sk 3 ch, *dc in the next 2 ch, (1 dc, ch 3, 1 dc) in the next ch, sk 1 ch*, dc in the last 3 ch, ch 3, turn.

Row 2. *(3 dc, ch 3, 1 sc) in each ch-3 sp*, 1 dc between last group of 3 dc and turning ch, ch 3, turn. Repeat from Row 2.

Pineapple Stitch

This stitch is the perfect representation of focused intention rising up toward the Ancients and Their blessings raining down upon us. Use it for bringing abstract wishes into reality, to receive the blessings of the deities in any effort, or to invoke Akasha.

Work the pineapple stitch on a multiple of two chains plus four and crochet as follows:

Row 1. Sk 3 ch, *1 pineapple [(yo, insert hook, draw up a loop) 4 times in same ch, yo, draw through 8 loops, yo, draw through the last 2 loops], ch 1, sk 1 ch*, 1 pineapple, ch 3, turn.

Row 2. *1 pineapple in each ch sp of previous row*, 1 pineapple in the turning ch sp, ch 3, turn. Repeat from Row 2.

Cluster Lace

Because of its airy, busy effect, cluster lace belongs to the Air deities. The stitch also forms an abstract iris design, so it holds the magic of the rainbow and often, messages from loved ones who have crossed over.

Work cluster lace on a multiple of six chains plus four and crochet as follows:

Row 1. Sk 3 ch *(1 dc, ch 2, 1 dc) in next ch, sk 2 ch 1 puff [(yo, insert hook, draw up a loop) 4 times in the same ch, yo, draw through 9 loops], ch 1, sk 2 ch*, (1 dc, ch 2, 1 dc) in last ch, ch 3, turn.

Row 2. *1 puff in ch-2 sp between 2 dc of previous row, ch 1 (1 dc, ch 2, 1 dc) under loop that closes the puff in previous row*, 1 puff, 1 dc in ch-3 sp at beginning of previous row, ch 3, turn.

Row 3. (1 dc, ch 2, 1 dc) in top of puff, *1 puff in ch-2 sp, ch 1 (1 dc, ch 2, 1 dc) in top of puff*, 1 dc in ch-3 sp at beginning of the previous row, ch 3, turn. Repeat from Row 2.

Magical Granny Squares: An Exercise in Versatility

Within the magical realm, granny squares are the most versatile of all crochet types. Nearly anything may be constructed from them and better yet, different motifs can be connected to form unique magical vibrations. Because every granny square begins from a small circle in the center, it is a true representation of the magician at work. When the individual vibrations of separate motifs combine with the power of the magician, the possibilities for enchantment are endless. Here are a few of the motifs that I find most magically potent.

Traditional Granny Square

The traditional granny combines the firmness of Earth with the solidity of the Ancients. A four-sided figure, it may be used to represent the total of the Elements in conjunction with the magician, for all works come from the center and manifest outward. Use this motif for any magical purpose. Basic instructions for this motif are as follows:

ROUND 1. Ch 6, join with slst to form a ring. Ch 3, 2 dc in ring, ch 2 (3 dc in ring, ch 2) 3 times, slst in top of beg ch-3.

ROUND 2. Ch 3, (2 dc, ch 2, 3 dc) in same sp to form corner, *ch 1, 3 dc, make corner*, join.

ROUND 3. Repeat Round 2, making 3 dc, ch 1 in every ch-1space.

Eyelet Square

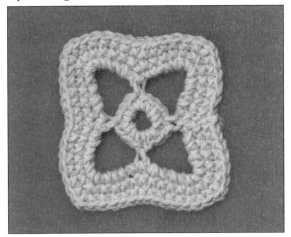

This motif is an excellent representation of the Elements. It also works well in efforts of psychic and mundane protection, as it has the ability to shield one from the "evil eye." Basic instructions for this motif are as follows:

ROUND 1. Wind yarn twice around finger to make ring, then make 16 sc in ring, joining with slst.

ROUND 2. (1 sc, ch 10, sk 3 sc) 4 times, slst in first sc.

ROUND 3. (11 sc in ch-10 sp, 1 sc in next st) 4 times, slst in first sc.

ROUND 4. *Sc in next 6 sts, 2 sc in next st to form corner, sc in next 5 sts* 3 times; slst in first sc.

ROUND 5. Sc in each st around, making 2 sc in each corner. End off.

Hexagon

Pinwheel

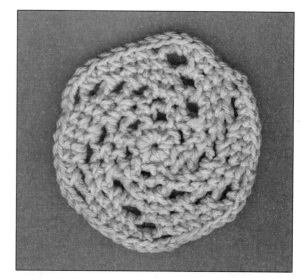

This six-sided motif leans toward romance, love, and harmony. It works well in efforts for the household or in projects such as afghans or bedspreads. Basic instructions for this motif are as follows:

ROUND 1. Ch 6, join to form a ring. Ch 2, 2 dc in ring, ch 3, (3 dc in ring, ch 3) 5 times, slst in top of beg ch.

ROUND 2. Ch 4, *(3 tr, ch 3, 3 tr) in each ch-3 sp* to last sp, then make 3 tr, ch 3, 2 tr and slst in top of beg ch.

ROUND 3. Ch 3, 1 dc in each tr and 2 dc, ch2 in each corner, slst in top of beg ch.

ROUND 4. Ch 3, sk 2 sts, dc in next st, dc in st behind st just worked, *sk 1 st, dc in next st, dc in skipped st* to end making ch-2 in corners; dc in st in front of beg ch-3, slst in top of beg ch.

The pinwheel is a delightful depiction of the magical circle—the six spokes symbolizing the four Quarters and the Lord and Lady, and the swirl of the spokes representing the spiral dance. Use it in efforts involving friendships, partnerships, and relationships. Basic instructions for this motif are as follows:

ROUND 1. Ch 4, slst to form a ring; 12 sc in ring.

ROUND 2. Sc in first st, *ch 3, sk next st, sc in next sc* to end. (Six ch-3 sps)

ROUND 3. Sc in ch-3 sp, *ch 3, sc in next st, sc in ch-3sp* ch 3, sk next sc, sc in next sc.

ROUND 4. 2 sc in ch-3 sp, *ch 3, sk next st, sc in next st, 2 sc in ch-3 sp* ch 3, sk next sc, sc in next two sc.

ROUND 5. 2 sc in ch-3 sp, *ch 3, sk next st, sc in next 2sc, 2 sc in ch-3 sp* ch 3, sk next sc, sc in each of next three sc.

ROUND 6. 2 sc in ch-3 sp, *ch 3, sk next st, sc in next 3 sts, 2 sc in ch-3 sp* ch 3, sk next sc, sc in each of next four sc. Fasten off.

Octagon

Because of its shape and the eight spokes in the center, the octagonal motif characterizes the Wheel of the Year. Basic instructions for this motif are as follows:

ROUND 1. Ch 6, join with slst to form ring. Ch 2, 23 dc in ring; join with slst to top of beg ch-2.

ROUND 2. Ch 4, dc in same st, ch 1 *sk 2 sts, (1 dc, ch 2, 1 dc) in next st, ch 1* to end; join with slst to 2nd ch of ch-4.

ROUND 3. Slst in first ch-2 sp, ch 2 in same ch-2 sp and make 1 dc, ch 2, 2 dc, *1 dc in next ch sp, (2 dc, ch 2, 2 dc) in next ch sp* to end; join with slst to top of ch-2.

ROUND 4. Sc in each st around, adding 2 sc in each ch sp; slst in first sc.

Popcorn

A nine-round, nine-puff popcorn design, this is a terrific motif to use in gaining favors or making wishes come to fruition. Basic instructions for this motif are as follows:

ROUND 1. Ch 5, join with slst to form a ring. Ch 3, 2 dc in ring, (ch 3, 3 dc in ring) 3 times, ch 3, join to top of beg ch-3 with slst.

ROUND 2. Ch 3, dc in each dc, making 2 dc, ch 3, 2 dc in each space. Join with slst to top of beg ch-3.

ROUND 3. Ch 3, *5 dc in the next dc; remove loop from hook, then insert it through the top of the first dc and the dropped loop, pulling the dropped loop through [popcorn made]; ch 1, dc in each dc, 2 dc, ch 3, 2dc in each corner space*, join to beg ch 3 with slst.

ROUND 4. Ch 3, *dc in popcorn and next dc, make popcorn in next dc, dc in next 3 dc, 2 dc, ch 3, 2 dc in next space, dc in next 3 dc, popcorn in next dc, dc in next st* to end, join to beg ch 3 with slst.

ROUND 5. Ch 3, *popcorn in next dc, dc in next 3 sts, pop-corn in next st, dc in next 3 sts, 2 dc, ch 3, 2 dc in corner sp, popcorn in next st, dc in next 3 sts* to end, join to beg ch 3 with slst.

ROUND 6. Repeat Round 5, only making 2 popcorns.

ROUND 7. Repeat Round 6, only making 1 popcorn.

ROUND 8. Repeat Round 7, but make no pop-corns.

ROUND 9. Dc around, making ch 3 in each corner; end off.

Wagon Wheel

A truly circular motif, the wagon wheel is a good depiction of the effects of karma. The rounds that work outward from the center characterize the rippling effect of a karmic stone thrown into the cosmic pond. Use it for past-life work, meditation, and projects involving unconditional love. Basic instructions for this motif are as follows:

ROUND 1. Ch 4, join to form ring. Ch 3, 1 petal in ring [(yo, insert hook, draw up a loop) twice, yo, draw through 5 loops, ch 1], 7 more petals in ring, slst in top of beg ch.

ROUND 2. Slst to first ch-sp, slst in ch-sp, ch 2, 1 dc in first ch sp, ch 2, (2 dc, ch2) in next 7 ch sps, slst in top of beg ch.

ROUND 3. Slst to first ch-sp, slst in ch-sp, ch 2, (1 dc, ch 1, 2 dc, ch 1) in first ch sp, (2 dc, ch 1, 2dc) in next 7 ch sps, slst in top of beg ch.

ROUND 4. Ch 2, 2 dc in first ch sp, ch 1 (3 dc, ch 1) in each of next 15 sps, fasten off.

Threads and Yarns: Natural Fiber Versus Man-Made Fiber

For as long as I can remember, the Pagan community has been in constant debate over the use of fibers for magical clothing and tools. Some practitioners believe that anything less than an all-natural fiber won't hold magical vibration. They contend that magical energy simply bounces off man-made fibers and scatters uncontrollably into the Universe. Others believe that once magical energy lives within a man-made fiber, it just lies there inertly. Their reasoning is that man-made fibers cannot "breathe" like natural ones.

Having worked many successful projects from both fiber types, I wonder at the basis for these charges. For example, cotton and flax plants must be chemically fertilized and treated with herbicides and pesticides to ensure a good crop. Once harvested by today's machinery, wool—like flax and cotton—is chemically cleaned, bleached, dyed, and "sized" to avoid unnecessary elasticity. To say that a fabric is all-natural by the time it arrives at the fabric store is really stretching the imagination. The only way to obtain such an item in today's world is to gather, clean, spin, and weave the fiber yourself.

Still have doubts? Here is some food for thought. In ancient times, magical people used ingredients readily available to them and only natural fibers were accessible. If those same people lived today, they would probably still practice their craft using easily available materials and give little or no thought to whether a fiber was "all-natural" or "man-made."

Although an all-natural yarn, thread, or fabric may be useful in magical needlework, there are many reasons you might wish to consider one that is man-made.

Allergies

I am allergic to unlined wool. Some people are also allergic to cotton, silk, and flax. Man-made fibers are generally hypo-allergenic. What good is a magical afghan or sweater if the recipient of your labors can't use it?

Availability and Expense

Because man-made fibers are usually hypo-allergenic, inexpensive, and easy to care for, there is a great demand for them in the retail market. This means synthetics will be easier to find, stocked in greater variety, and less expensive than all-natural fibers. Just remember: extra expense does not necessarily make your magic more effective.

Cleaning

Today's fibers are much easier to care for, and rolling precious items in layers of absorbent terrycloth is no longer necessary. If your magical items get dirty, a quick toss in the washer and dryer solves the problem.

Ecology

Using man-made fibers is ecologically effective, and, to those in the Pagan community, that should be a definite plus. These yarns and threads often come from recycled plastics (see the explanation in the Chapter Three)—the same plastics that clutter our beloved Earth and refuse to disintegrate. By using these fibers in your magical projects, you do your part to preserve the Earth Mother's legacy for future generations.

Walking the ancient paths should not make our lives more difficult; our paths should unwind easily before us and lead us to peace and joy. I am not encouraging the disposal of ancient rituals or suggesting that natural materials be thoroughly disregarded in the workings of magical needlecraft. I'm only advocating a bit of modern thinking and suggesting that you try some of the synthetic wonders available to you. I think you will be pleasantly surprised with the finished result. Not only will those fibers give added life to your completed project, the Earth Mother will thank you for your efforts to keep Her safe and clean.

Crocheted Tarot Card Bag

Project design by Dorothy Morrison.

This pattern works well for standard-size decks such as Morgan Greer or Arthurian. Try using shades of violet in creating this bag, as it is the color of psychic development and power. Alternative color schemes might include the colors of the Elements, white to symbolically light your path, or green for growth—especially if you are using the Tarot for guidance or as a teaching tool.

While making this bag, keep its purpose in mind. Visualize the bag protecting your cards, keeping them safe from negative influences and preserving their magical power.

Materials

size I crochet hook

½ ounce deep violet knitting worsted

½ ounce medium violet knitting worsted

½ ounce light violet knitting worsted

tapestry needle

1⅓ yard ⅛" deep violet ribbon or satin cord

To Make the Tarot Card Bag

Back

ROUND 1. Beginning at the center of the back with deep violet, ch 16. 2dc in the 4th ch from hook, ch 3, 3dc in same ch (sk 3 ch, 3dc in next ch) 3 times, (ch 3, 3dc in same as last 3dc) twice, working on opposite side of starting ch, (sk 3 ch, 3dc in next ch) 3 times, ch 3, slst in top of ch- 3 at beg of round. End off.

ROUND 2. Join medium violet in first ch-3 sp of Round 1, ch 3, 2dc in same sp, ch 3, 3dc in same sp, (3dc in next sp between groups of 3dc) 3 times, 3dc, ch 3, 3dc in next ch-3 sp, 3dc, ch 3, 3dc in center dc of next group, 3dc, ch 3, 3dc in next ch-3 sp, (3dc in next sp between groups of 3dc) 3 times, 3dc, ch 3, 3dc in corner ch-3 sp, slst in top of ch-3 at beg of round. End off.

ROUND 3. Join light violet in first ch-3 sp of Round 2, ch 3, 2dc in same sp, ch 3, 3dc in same sp, (3dc in next sp) 4 times, (3dc, ch 3, 3dc in next ch-3 sp, 3dc in next sp between groups of 3dc) 3 times, (3dc in next sp) 4 times, 3dc, ch 3, 3dc in corner ch-3 sp, 3dc in next sp, slst in top of ch-3 at beg of round. End off.

ROUND 4. Join medium violet in first ch-3 sp of Round 3, ch 3, 2dc in same sp, (3dc in next sp) 8 times, 3dc, ch 3, 3dc in next point, (3dc in next sp) 8 times, 3dc, ch 3, 3dc in corner ch-3 sp, (3dc in next sp) twice, slst in top of ch-3 at beg of round. End off.

Front

ROUND 1. Beginning with deep violet at the center, ch 16. Repeat Round 1. End off.

ROUND 2. Join medium violet in first ch-3 sp of Round 1, ch 3, 2dc, ch 3, 3dc in same sp, (3dc in next sp) 3 times, (3dc, ch 3, 3dc in next sp) twice, (3dc in next sp) 3 times, 3dc, ch 3, 3dc in corner sp, slst in top of ch-3 at beg of round. End off.

ROUND 3. Join light violet in first ch-3 sp of Round 2, ch 3, 2dc in same sp, (3dc in next sp) 4 times, 3dc, ch 3, 3dc in corner ch-3 sp, 3dc in next sp, 3dc in corner ch-3 sp, (3dc in next sp) 5 times. End off.

ROUND 4. Join medium violet in first ch-3 of Round 3, ch 3, dc in next 17 sts, 3dc, ch 3, 3dc in corner sp, dc in next 9 sts, 3dc, ch 3, 3dc in corner sp, dc in last 18 sts. End off.

Finishing

Thread the tapestry needle with medium violet. Right sides facing and square ends matched, sew the sides and bottom together, leaving the opening at the top free. Turn the bag inside out. Cut the ribbon in half and holding both pieces together, tie it in the center of the deep violet stitches on the front of bag. Thread the ends through the spaces just above the flap point and tie in a bow.

After you have finished, consecrate the bag to Ashtaroth by chanting:

Bless this bag to hold my cards—
Negative energy from it ward!
Let it insulate the Tarot's power!
Protection grow with every hour!

Goddess Bag

Project design by Elayne of Wichita, Kansas.

These bags have many magical functions, but one of the most interesting is in the "Purging Ceremony." For this ritual, fill the bag with symbols of old habits, past hurts, wounds, and unfortunate experiences. Tie it up and either bury it in the earth or toss it into a running body of water. Use the following chant during the bag disposal process:

Bag of hurt, of habit and pain!
Kill your contents with disdain!
Eradicate them one and all!
Let only joy upon me fall!

It is a great ritual that, used from time to time, enriches everyone's lives.

Materials

size 7 steel crochet hook

crochet thread

½ yard ¼" ribbon

To Make the Goddess Bag

ROUND 1. Ch 30; sc in second ch from hook, sc in each ch across, ending with 3 sc in last ch. Working on opposite side of foundation ch, sc in each ch across, ending with 2 sc in last ch; slst to join, ch 1.

ROUND 2. Sc in each sc around, join; ch 1.

ROUND 3. Repeat Round 2.

ROUND 4. Sc in each sc around, working in back loops only, join; ch 1.

ROUND 5. Repeat Round 2.

ROUND 6. Repeat Round 4.

ROUNDS 7–9. Repeat Round 2.

ROUND 10. Repeat Round 2, join; ch 2. Continue with rounds of hdc until bag is 4½ to 5 inches long; ch 5.

NEXT ROUND. *Sk 2 sts, dc in next st, ch 3* to end, join; ch 1.

NEXT ROUND. *Sc, dc, sc* in each loop across, join; ch 1.

LAST ROW. Sc in each st across, join; fasten off.

Finishing

Weave ribbon through the loops at the top of bag for closing.

The Thirteen Ring Motif
(Altar Cloth Border or Ceremonial Neckpiece)

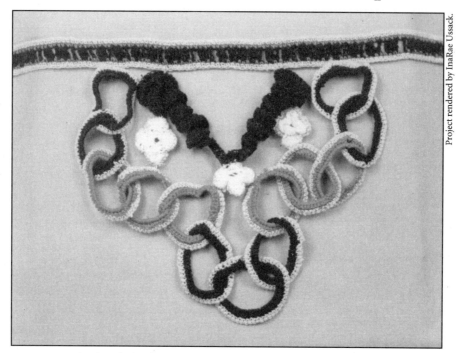

Project design by InaRae Ussack of **Craft/Crafts Magazine.**

This magical delight came from the modification of a British pattern of the 1800s. As the pattern is a symbolic representation of the thirteen Moons in each year, this design makes a perfect border for an altar cloth. For those of you who don't work with altar cloths, the pattern also works up beautifully as a ceremonial "collar," and may be used as a piece of ritual jewelry. Feel free to substitute colors if other shades better suit your magical needs.

Materials

    size 7 crochet hook
1   225 ball of black crochet cotton
1   225 ball of gold crochet cotton
1   225 ball of red crochet cotton
    a small amount of white crochet cotton
    sewing thread in matching colors

To Make the Thirteen Ring Motif

Beginning

With black ch 34. Join with slst to form a ring.

ROUND 1. FIRST RING. Work 48 sc in the ring.

ROUND 2. Working in back loops only, sc in each sc around, fasten off.

ROUND 3. With gold, in back thread only, sc in each sc around, fasten off.

Second Ring

With black, ch 34, pass the end of the ch upward through the first ring and join. Continue as for first ring.

Subsequent Rings

Continue as for second ring, noting that the third, fourth, and fifth rings are of red, and the sixth is again of black. After completing the sixth ring, make a second chain of rings exactly like you did the first. You will have two chains of rings with six rings in each.

Thirteenth Ring

(This ring forms the point at the bottom of the motif and is a little larger than the others.) With black, ch 40, take the end of the ch upward through the last black ring of the right side of the motif and downward through the last ring of the left hand side, join to form a circle. Work 54 sc in the circle and complete it in the same fashion as the others.

FLOWER. With white, ch 6, join with slst to form ring.

ROUND 1. In the first st make: 1 sc, 2hdc, 2dc, 2 tr, 2dc, 2hdc, 2sc, then work 1 sc in the circle (one petal made). Repeat 3 times (4 petals).

ROUND 2. Keeping the petals to the front, sc in the back of sc of the last round, ch 4 and slst under next sc until you have 4 ch loops.

ROUND 3. In each loop make 2dc, 5tr, 3dc then sc, and repeat around for 4 petals. Fasten off.

ROUND 4. With gold, slst in sc, then sc in each st around. Fasten off.

Make two more flowers the same color, for a total of three flowers.

Horns

With black, ch 37, dc in 4th ch from hook, dc in the next 5 ch, make 5 dc in each of the next 10 chs. Make 5 tr in each of the next 10 chs, make dtr in the remaining chs. One side of horns completed, repeat for the second side of horns.

Heading

With black, make a chain the desired length (the length of your altar cloth or the length you'd like for the ceremonial neckpiece).

ROUND 1. Dc in 4th ch from hook and in next ch. Sk one ch, dc in the next ch, sk one ch, dc in the next 2 chs across. Fasten off.

ROUND 2. With red, sc in each st around with three sts at the corners to keep work flat. Fasten off.

ROUND 3. Repeat Round 2, this time with gold. Fasten off.

Finishing

Using a damp cloth to protect your work, iron the rings and heading, keeping rings round and flat. Consecrate and bless the ritual piece by saying:

> **Ever mind the Law of Three—**
> **And Maiden, Mother, Crone—in me!**
> **May magic manifest in thee!**
> **As I will, so mote it be!**

Cat and Pentagram Filet Crochet Vest

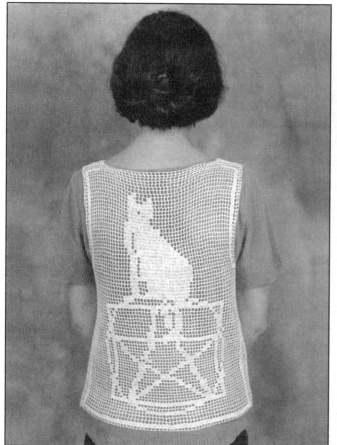
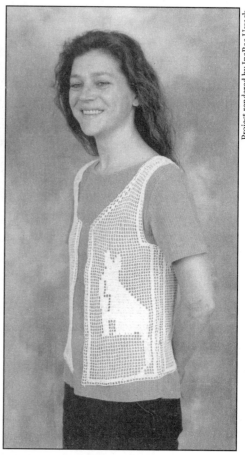

Project rendered by InaRae Ussack.

Project design by InaRae Ussack of Craft/Crafts Magazine.

This magical vest is terrific for wearing over your robe in Circle or out on the street. It holds the power of the pentagram, the femininity of the circle, and the masculinity and Element power of the square. The cat—sacred to Bast and long thought the symbol of the Witch—adds instinctual cleverness and creativity to any magical working.

Materials

750 yards crochet cotton #30 (yardage approximate)

size 9 steel crochet hook or size to make gauge

Gauge: 4" square = 14 meshes by 17 rows.

Abbreviations

OM   Open MesFh: dc, ch2, dc.

SM   Solid Mesh: 4dc.

128 ▸•◦────────   *Magical Crochet: Chaining the Magic*

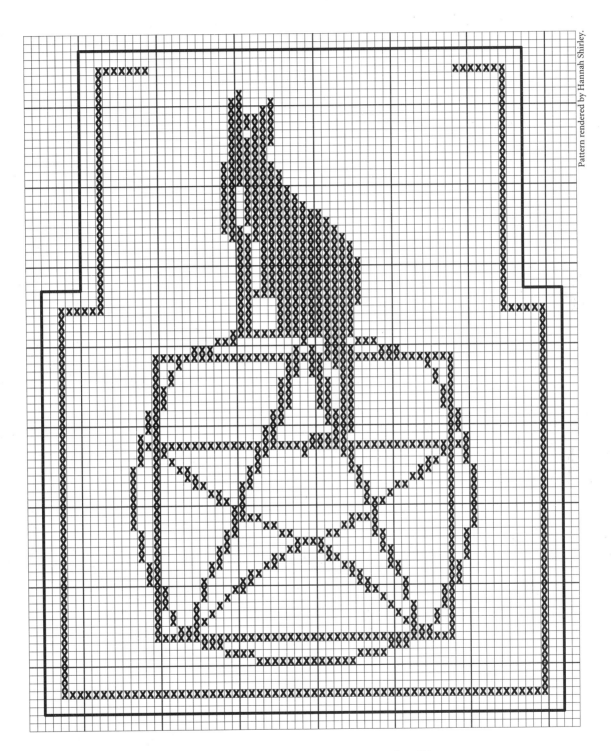

Pattern rendered by Hannah Shirley.

Cat and Pentagram Vest pattern (back).

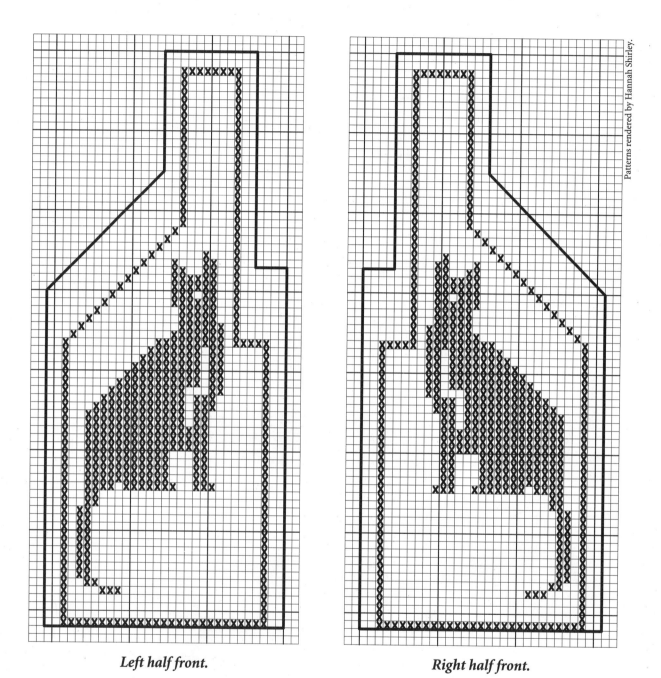

Left half front.

Right half front.

Cat and Pentagram Vest pattern (front).

To Make the Cat and Pentagram Vest

Sizing

The directions for this vest are for a person with a 32-inch bust size. To increase the size of the pattern, increase the number of meshes and rows. For example, for a 36-inch bust, add two or three meshes to both sides of each piece. For each size increase, add nine rows of open mesh to the top and bottom of each piece. Don't forget to purchase more crochet thread if you are planning a larger size.

Back

Ch 197 plus 5 to turn. (3ch = dc and 2ch = first open mesh)

Row 1. Dc in 9th ch from hook *ch2, sk 2 sts, dc in next st, repeat from * across. 65 OM.

Row 2. 2 OM, 61 SM, 2 OM.

Rows 3 through 50. Follow pattern.

Row 51. To decrease at the beginning of Row 51, slst across first 5 OM; at the end of row, decrease by leaving 5 OM unworked.

Left Half Front

Ch 95.

Row 1. 31 OM.

Row 2. 2 OM, 27 SM, 2 OM.

Rows 3 through 50. Follow pattern.

Row 51. To decrease for neck edge, dec 1 mesh on each row for 15 rows, while simultaneously dec 1 mesh for armhole (as you did for the back). Then work evenly for 18 rows. Fasten off.

Right Half Front

Work as for the left half front, following the graph for the right half front.

Finishing

Sew shoulder and side seams with small overhand stitches. Press lightly with steam iron, then enchant with the following verse:

> Oh, power of pentagram! Steadfastness of square!
> Magic of Circle and enchantment found there!
> Heighten my instincts! Creativity flow!
> Within, without, above and below!

Crocheted Necklace Pouch

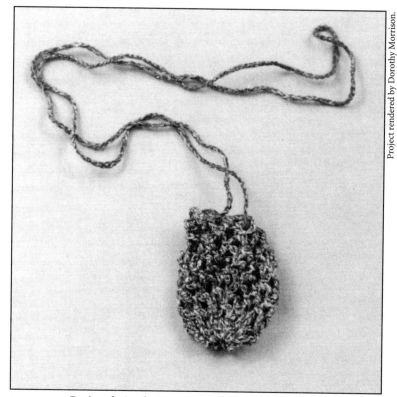

Project rendered by Dorothy Morrison.

Project design by Mayrose of Carbondale, Illinois.

You can make a beautiful charm bag with the two simplest crochet stitches—chain and slip stitch. What makes this pouch so special is the colorful mixture of threads used. The result is so pretty that the bag will likely double as your favorite fashion accessory.

Materials

	size 7 steel crochet hook
5–7	spools of colored sewing thread
1	large tapestry needle
1	small tapestry needle

super glue or clear nail polish

smooth bowl to house the spools while you work with them

Note About the Thread

At least four strands of thread should be cotton, cotton covered polyester, polyester, or silk, as they add strength. The remaining threads may be rayon, metallic, or polyester metallic blending filament; however, you may wish to experiment before you begin as some metallic threads may be too stiff to work easily.

To Make the Necklace Pouch

Pouch

ROUND 1. Leaving a tail about ten inches long, ch 10, slst in beg ch to make a ring.

ROUND 2. Ch 5, slst through ring to make a scallop. Repeat to make 14 scallops, then slide them around to even out the spacing. Slst 2 up the first scallop, then work one slst in the top of the scallop.

ROUND 3. Ch 5, slst in the next scallop and continue around; slst to the top of the first scallop to start a new row.

ROUNDS 4 THROUGH 11. Repeat Round 3.

ROUND 12. Slst in each st of previous round. At end, cut ten inches of un-crocheted thread and pull through the last st.

Drawstring

Grasp the ends of all thread strands except the metallic and slowly draw them out until they are the length of your outstretched arms. Do not cut, but grasp at that point until you have three arm-reaches of thread piled in your lap.

Add back a single strand of metallic thread and make a chain, continuing to work until you have used the entire pile in your lap. Leave a five inch tail on both ends.

Finishing

Thread the ending tail of the bag into the small tapestry needle and sew it down the spine you created by the slsts you made. Bring out from the ring that forms the foundation for the second round. Let that tail hang and thread the beginning tail into the needle. Sew it through the ring, going around several times, drawing it up as tight as you can. Put a dab of Super

Glue or clear nail polish on each tail where it emerges from the fabric. Let it harden and snip the ends off. Turn the bag right side out.

Thread one tail of the drawstring chain into the big tapestry needle and weave it in and out through the top round of the scallops of the bag (see Figures C-1 and C-2).

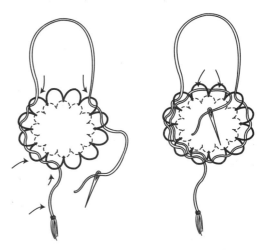

FIGURE C-1.   FIGURE C-2.

Knot both together, trim them evenly, and let them hang as fringe down the front of the bag. Close the bag by tugging on the loop that hangs around the neck (Figure C-3).

FIGURE C-3.

Stone/Crystal Cups

Project design by Elayne of Wichita, Kansas.

Use these cups to hold your favorite stones. Being small, they are the perfect housing for the crystals on your desk at the workplace or even for stones you use on your altar. This project is so quick, easy, and inexpensive to construct, it also makes the perfect gift.

Materials

size 7 steel crochet hook

size 10 crochet thread

To Make the Cups

ROUND 1. Ch 4, slst to form a ring; ch 1.

ROUND 2. 7 sc in ring, join; ch 1.

ROUND 3. 2 sc in each st around, join; ch 1.

ROUND 4. Sc in same st, *sc in next st, 2 sc in next st* around to end, join; ch 1.

ROUND 5. Repeat Round 4.

ROUND 6. Sc in same st, *sc in next 3 sts, 2 sc in next st* round to end, join; ch 1.

ROUND 7. Sc in same st, *sc in next 4 sts, 2 sc in next st* around to end, join; ch 1.

ROUND 8. Sc in same st, *sc in next 5 sts, 2 sc in next st* around to end, join; ch 1.

ROUND 9. Working in back loops only, sc in each st around to end, join; ch 1. Continue working Round 9 until the cup is the height you want it to be.

Magical Crochet: Chaining the Magic

ROUND 10. *Ch 3, sk one st, slst in next st* around to end, join; ch 1.

ROUND 11. Slst in first ch-3 sp, *ch 3, slst in next ch-3 sp* around to end, join; ch 1.

LAST ROUND. Slst in first loop, *3 sc in next loop, slst in next loop* around to end, join; fasten off.

Enchant the finished stone holder by blessing it with the Elements. Add the stones to the cup and chant:

Oh little cup of sturdy thread,
Act now both as home and bed,
For the stones which I hold dear—
Protect them while they dwell in here!

Pentacle Wallhanging

Project rendered by Cindy Hatcher.

Project design by Dorothy Morrison.

This beautiful filet-crocheted wallhanging or altar cloth is based on a counted cross stitch pattern designed by Alodi of Field-N-Forest. The pattern is very versatile and may also be used a decorative table runner.

Materials

    size 7 steel crochet hook

1 large ball crochet cotton

Abbreviations

    OM Open Mesh: trc, ch2, trc.

    SM Solid Mesh: 4dc.

Pentacle Wallhanging pattern.

To Make the Pentacle Wallhanging

Row 1. Ch 219, trc in 6th ch from hook and in each ch across; ch 5, turn.

Row 2. Sk first trc, trc in next 3 trc, *ch 2, sk 2 trc, trc in next trc* to last 3 trc, trc in last 3 trc; ch 5, turn.

Rows 3 and 4. Repeat Row 2.

Row 5; End. Follow the graph to the end, making SM where the x's are marked and OM in the blanks.

Suggested Sources for Specialty Threads and Yarns

Spring House Yarns
649 Wexford Bayne Road
Wexford, PA 15090
(412) 935-5266

Send $1.50 for current catalogue and price list.

Straw Into Gold, Inc.
3006 San Pablo Avenue
Berkeley, CA 94702
(415) 548-5241

Send $.45 postage and self-addressed, stamped envelope for current catalogue.

Tatsy
P.O. Box 1401
Des Plaines, IL 60018

Send $1 for current catalogue.

Turn of the Century
1676 Millsboro Road E.
Mansfield, OH 44906
(419) 529-TURN

Send self-addressed, stamped envelope for current price list. This company specializes in wooden hooks and other miscellaneous needlework tools.

Suggested Sources for Alternative Patterns

Miss Chiff
Misc. by Miss Chiff
10131 East 32nd St., Apt. C
Tulsa, OK 74146-1405

InaRae Ussack
Craft/Crafts Magazine
P.O. Box 441
Ponderay, ID 83852

Suggested Reading List

McCall's Big Book of Needlecrafts (ABC Needlework and Crafts Magazines, Inc., 1982). Published in 1989 by Chilton Book Company, Radnor, Penn.; published in 1989 by VNR Publishers, Scarborough, Ontario, Canada.

Mildred Graves Ryan, *The Complete Encyclopedia of Stitchery* (Garden City, N.Y.: Doubleday & Company, Inc., 1979).

Magical
Knitting
Connecting the Magic

Chapter Six

I was six years old when I learned to knit. My older sister came home from school one day and proudly announced that one of her teachers had shown her how. There was an immediate trip to the five and dime for my own pair of needles so I could learn, too. Before long, I was knitting away and thought I was the brightest child in the world.

After the first thirty minutes, I told my mother that I had practiced enough and was ready for a real project. Though I had grandiose ideas of knitting an entire wardrobe and at least a hundred other niceties, Mama finally burst my bubble by telling me that I should knit something small and simple like an afghan. I insisted upon making at least a bedspread. The only thing we did agree upon was that the project should take the form of garter stitch blocks. I hadn't yet learned how to purl.

For the rest of the spring and a good portion of the summer I knitted the blocks, and Mama carefully tucked them away in an old dress box. School came 'round again and I forgot all about the project. In fact, it never crossed my mind until about fifteen years ago, when the postman delivered a large package from my mother. Inside its brown paper wrapping was an afghan made from the blocks I had knitted so many years before. A note attached read:

I found these when I cleaned the cedar chest, so I sat down and put them together for you. As I worked, memories of the excited little girl who made them came back. I remembered the look on her face, glowing with accomplishment when she'd finished one. Seeing the mistakes, I remembered the crease in her brow as she struggled to make each one perfect.

Finishing this afghan brought back precious memories of the precocious and delightful little girl who is now so very grown-up and poised. I hope this afghan brings you the same joy of magical remembrance that it did for me.

Love,
Mama

Magically speaking, knitting holds the same enchantment vibration as weaving, except that no loom is necessary, and the artist uses two "shuttles" (the needles) instead of one. Knitting is the harmonious "connector" and works to promote relationships, networking, and business. It certainly worked well in the afghan project that my mother finished for me. At the time, Mama and I weren't seeing eye to eye on anything and the completion of the afghan seemed to change all that. It marked a badly needed turning point in our relationship.

Just as knitting connects, unraveling knitting symbolizes separation. For example, if you want to break a bad habit or remove yourself peacefully from a distasteful relationship, tightly knit a piece of cloth of nine rows to connect all the negativity present. Then each day for nine days, unravel one row of fabric while asking the Lord and Lady to remove the dilemma from your life. Each day, the problems decrease and the situation improves. The results are amazing!

The Magical Basics of Knitting and Purling

Only two basic stitches are used in this art-form: knitting and purling.

The **knit stitch** is the bringer of harmony. It is formed by twirling the yarn deosil (clockwise) over a needle in the back to make a new stitch and slipping the old one off the other needle to form a ridge on the back side. Its energy flow is even and smooth, slow and determined, balanced and certain. It is the soft strength of the Goddess at Her most creative and represents the pure harmony of Her being.

The **purl stitch** represents adhesion. Wrapping the yarn widdershins (counter-clockwise) over a needle in the front creates this stitch. Unlike knitting, purling causes a ridge to form on the side of the fabric facing you. The energy vibrating from the purl stitch is strong and vital, vigorous and enthusiastic, potent and intense. It is the masculine force of the God at the height His virility and symbolizes the power of His eternal connection to the Goddess.

When you work alternating rows of each stitch, the **stockinette stitch** comes to life. Because it is totally balanced, it not only connects people, ideas, and values but does so with complete and symmetrical harmony. Smooth on one side and ridged on the other, it represents the Child born of the union of the Lord and Lady.

I have listed several stitches and stitch patterns that hold magical meaning for me. Though some of them may look difficult at first glance, they are all relatively simple. If you can knit and purl, you can work each of the following patterns quickly and adeptly.

Stitch Abbreviations

The following abbreviations are used throughout the instructions for the following magical stitches and in the instructions for the magical crochet projects in this chapter.

K (knit), p (purl), st (stitch), dp (double-pointed), sl (slip), psso (pass slipped stitch or stitches over), yo (yarn over).

Magical Knitting Stitches and Patterns

Garter Stitch

Formed by knitting each row, the garter stitch is the simplest of all stitches. Though ridges form on both sides of the fabric, a smooth line of stitches lies between each row. This configuration makes the garter stitch a good representation of the marriage of the Lord and Lady and perfect balance.

Rib Stitch

This stitch forms straight rows within the fabric—one smooth and raised; the other recessed and ridged. The rib stitch may be used to symbolize the paths in your life. If your paths haven't been especially smooth or straight, increase the number of knit stitches within your magical project to keep your feet off shaky ground.

Form the rib stitch by casting on a multiple of six stitches plus three and working in the following manner:

Row 1. K 3, *p 3, k 3* to end.

Row 2. P 3, *k 3, p 3* to end.

Lattice Stitch

The lattice stitch forms a very heavy, sturdy knit. Use it in projects where strong connections are necessary. The lattice stitch is excellent for magical endeavors involving tight-knit groups, business matters, or for efforts relating to moral support.

Form the lattice stitch by casting on a multiple of six stitches and working in the following manner:

Row 1. *K 4, p 2* to end.

Row 2. K the p sts and p the k sts of the previous row.

Row 3. *Slip 2 sts onto a double-pointed needle and leave at the back of work, k 2, k the 2 sts on dp needle, p 2* to end.

Row 4. Repeat Row 2.

Row 5. P 2, * k 2, slip 2 sts onto dp needle and leave at the back of work, k 2, p the 2 sts on the dp needle*; end with k 4.

Row 6. Repeat Row 2.

Row 7. *P 2, slip 2 sts onto dp needle and leave at the front, k 2, k the 2 sts on the dp needle* to end.

Row 8. Repeat Row 2.

Row 9. K 4, *slip 2 sts onto dp needle and leave at the front, p 2, k the 2 sts on the dp needle, k2*; end with p 2. Repeat Rows 2 through 9 for pattern.

Lozenge Stitch

This is a wonderful stitch to use when balance is the issue. Because it forms rough and smooth triangles equidistantly within a square, its symmetry is perfect. Use it in efforts intended to connect the mundane self with the magical self and to balance the total personality. As a triangular shape forms in the pattern, the lozenge stitch may also serve to represent the Triple Goddess and Triple God.

Form the lozenge stitch by casting on a multiple of five stitches and working in the following manner:

Row 1. *P 1, k 4* to end.

Row 2. *P 3, k 2* to end.

Row 3. Repeat Row 2.

Row 4. Repeat Row 1.

Row 5. Repeat Row 4.

Row 6. *K 2, p 3* to end.

Row 7. Repeat Row 6.

Row 8. *K 4, p 1* to end.

Florette Stitch

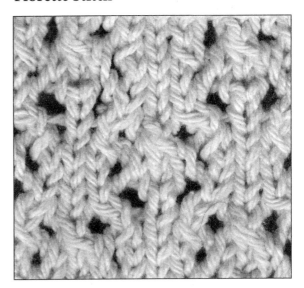

The florette stitch is a delightful representation of Goddess energy. Its soft curves and bell-shaped flowers symbolize all that is feminine. Use it in projects to represent the Goddess, fruitfulness, and abundance, or in those efforts that require a firm but gentle connective vibration.

Form the florette stitch by casting on a multiple of six stitches plus five and working in the following manner:

Row 1. P across.

Row 2. K 2, *p 1, yo, sl 1, k 1, psso, k 1, k 2 tog, yo*; end with k 3.

Row 3. P across.

Row 4. K4, *yo, k 3*; end with k 1.

Row 5. P across.

Row 6. K 2, k 2 tog, *yo, sl 1, k 1, psso, k 1, k 2 tog, yo, sl 2 knitwise (insert needle as if you were going to knit, then slip the sts to the next needle), k 1, psso*; end with yo, sl 1, k 1, psso, k 1, k2 tog, yo, sl 1, k 1, psso, k 2.

Row 7. P across.

Row 8. K 2, *k 1, k 2 tog, yo, k 1, yo, sl 1, k 1, psso*;end with k 3.

Row 9. P across.

Row 10. Repeat Row 4.

Row 11. P across.

Row 12. K 2, *k 1, k 2 tog, yo, sl 2 knitwise, k 1, psso, yo, sl 1, k 1, psso*; end with k 3.

Pine Trees Stitch

The pine trees stitch represents the earthy and virile energy of the God. It is best used in magical efforts concerning environmental issues and Nature, matters of spiritual growth, and putting oneself in tune with all other life forms. Pine trees is also an excellent stitch for those projects which require strength of conviction.

Form the pine trees pattern by casting on a multiple of fourteen stitches plus one and working in the following manner:

Row 1. K 1, *yo, k 2, p 3, p 3 tog, p 3, k 2, yo, k 1*.

Row 2. *P 4, k 7, p 3*; end with p 1.

Row 3. K1, * k1, yo, k 2, p 2, p 3 tog, p 2, k 2, yo, k 2*.

Row 4. *P 5, k 5, p 4*; end with p 1.

Row 5. K 1, *k2, yo, k 2, p 1, p 3 tog, p 1, k 2, yo, k 3*.

Row 6. *P 6, k 3, p 5*; end with p 1.

Row 7. K 1, *k 3, yo, k 2, p 3 tog, k 2, yo, k 4*.

Row 8. *P 7, k 1, p 6*; end with p 1.

Row 9. K 1, *k 4, yo, k 1, sl 1, k 2 tog, psso, k 1, yo, k 5*.

Row 10. P across.

Row 11. K 1, *k 5, yo, sl 1, k 2 tog, psso, yo, k 6*.

Row 12. P across.

Escalator Stitch

This stitch forms a pattern on the fabric that looks like stairs. Escalator is a wonderful stitch to use for any magical goal.

Form the escalator stitch by casting on a multiple of thirty-two stitches and working in the following manner:

Row 1. *K 5, p 11* to end.

Row 2. *K 11, p 5* to end.

Row 3. Repeat Row 1.

Row 4. P across.

Row 5. K across.

Row 6. P across.

Row 7. P 4, *k 5, p 11*; end with k 5, p 7.

Row 8. K 7, *p 5, k 11*; end with p 5, k 4.

Row 9. Repeat Row 7.

Row 10. P across.

Row 11. K across.

Row 12. P across.

Row 13. P 8, *k 5, p 11*; end with k 5, p 3.

Row 14. K 3, *P 5, k 11*; end with p 5, k 8.

Row 15. Repeat Row 13.

Row 16. P across.

Row 17. K across.

Row 18. P across.

Row 19. K 1, p 11, *k 5, p 11*; end with k 4.

Row 20. P 4, *k 11, p 5*; end with k 11, p 1.

Row 21. Repeat Row 19.

Row 22. P across.

Row 23. K across.

Row 24. P across.

Candle Stitch

This beautiful stitch looks much like the flame of the candle and belongs to the Fire Element. Use it to invoke the powers of that Element and add a spark of warmth to relationships. It is excellent when used for magical projects involving love.

Form the candle stitch by casting on a multiple of ten stitches plus one and working in the following manner:

Row 1. K3, *k 2 tog, yo, k 1, yo, sl 1, k 1, psso, k 5*; ending with k 3.

Row 2. P across.

Row 3. K2, *k 2 tog, k 1, yo, k1, yo, k1, sl 1, k 1, psso, k 3*; ending with k 2.

Row 4. P across.

Row 5. K1, *k 2 tog, k 2, yo, k1, yo, k 2, sl 1, k 1, psso, k 1*.

Row 6. P across.

Row 7. K 2 tog, *k 3, yo, k 1, yo, k 3, sl 1, k 2 tog, psso the 2 sts which are knitted tog*; ending with sl 1, k 1, psso.

Row 8. P across.

Row 9. K 1, *yo, sl 1, k 1, psso, k 5, k 2 tog, yo, k 1*.

Row 10. P across.

Row 11. K 1, *yo, k 1, sl 1, k 1, psso, , k 3, k 2 tog, k 1, yo, k 1*.

Row 12. P across.

Row 13. K 1, *yo, k 2, sl 1, k 1, psso, k 1, k 2 tog, k 2, yo, k 1*.

Row 14. P across.

Row 15. K 1, *yo, k 3, sl 1, k 2 tog, psso the 2 sts which are knitted tog, k 3, yo, k 1*.

Row 16. P across.

Chevron Stitch

The chevron stitch, because of its sharp waves, is akin to the Water Element. Use it in efforts involving emotional expression, attachment and connection, healing, tranquility, and peace.

Form the chevron stitch pattern by casting on a multiple of eight stitches plus one and working in the following manner:

Row 1. K 1, *p 7, k 1* to end.

Row 2. P 1, *k 7, p 1* to end.

Row 3. K 2, *p 5, k 3*; ending with p 5, k 2.

Row 4. P 2, *k 5, p 3*; ending with k 5, p 2.

Row 5. K 3, *p 3, k 5*; ending with p 3, k 3.

Row 6. P 3, *k 3, p 5*; ending with k 3, p 3.

Row 7. K 4, *p 1, k 7*; ending with p 1, k 4.

Row 8. P 4, *k 1, p 7*; ending with k 1, p 4.

Row 9. Repeat Row 2.

Row 10. Repeat Row 1.

Row 11. Repeat Row 4.

Row 12. Repeat Row 3.

Row 13. Repeat Row 6.

Row 14. Repeat Row 5.

Row 15. Repeat Row 8.

Row 16. Repeat Row 7.

Eyelet Lace Stitch

Eyelet lace is a delightful stitch with many magical uses. Because of its breezy and lacy look, it is an excellent representation of the Air Element. Because its pattern has the look of many "eyes," it is a great stitch to use in projects involving psychic protection and divination. Eyelet lace also works well in efforts to gain connection to the creative arts. (Note: Work this pattern very loosely, otherwise, you may have trouble when purling four together.)

Form eyelet lace by casting on a multiple of four stitches and working in the following manner:

Row 1. P 2, *yo, p 4 tog*; ending with yo, p 2.

Row 2. K 2, *K 1, p 1, k 1 in next yo, k 1*; ending with k 2.

Row 3. K across.

Block Stitch

What better stitch than blocks to symbolize the Earth? Solid squares of ridged and smooth texture alternate across the fabric. Use this stitch in efforts requiring stability, firmness, and strength.

Form the block stitch by casting on a multiple of ten stitches plus five and working in the following manner:

Row 1. K 5, *p 5, k 5* to end.

Row 2. P 5, *k 5, p 5* to end.

Row 3. Repeat Row 1.

Row 4. Repeat Row 2.

Row 5. Repeat Row 1.

Row 6. Repeat Row 1.

Row 7. Repeat Row 2.

Row 8. Repeat Row 1.

Row 9. Repeat Row 2.

Row 10. Repeat Row 1.

Diamond Brocade Stitch

Use diamond brocade in all magical efforts involving prosperity, financial gain, and business matters. It is also useful in projects that involve the expansion of support or networking of any type.

Form the diamond brocade stitch by casting on a multiple of six stitches plus one and working in the following manner:

Row 1. K 3, *p 1, k 5*; ending with p 1, k 3.

Row 2. P 2, *k 1, p 1, k1, p 3*; ending with k 1, p 1, k 1, p 2.

Row 3. *K 1, p 1, k 3, p 1*, ending with k 1.

Row 4. *K 1, p 5*; ending with k 1.

Row 5. Repeat Row 3.

Row 6. Repeat Row 2.

Casting On Begins the Spell

Casting on is the "base" of all knitting. In the magical sense, it is also the foundation from which any spell or effort of enchantment grows. For gentle spellworkings, casting on loosely is best. If you want to convey forceful energy, you may want to tighten the stitches somewhat as you work them. No matter how you begin, remember that casting on is the base from which the magic feeds, so be sure that the stitches are cast evenly and surely upon the needle.

As you form the initial stitches on the needle, keep in mind the purpose of your project and focus on it intently. For example, if you are beginning a project to bring other Pagans into your life, you may wish to chant something simple like:

**Pagans come from here and there—
Pagans greet me everywhere!**

Chanting as you cast on sets the mood and announces the goal for the spellworking. Telling the Universe specifically what you want is very important in any type of magical effort, because though the Universe never refuses to assist you, it only brings to you that for which you ask.

The story of the monkey's paw comes to mind here. A poor couple was granted several wishes through a severed monkey's paw, and their first wish was for money. Well, they got exactly what they asked for—they were the beneficiaries of their only son's life insurance policy.

This grisly example demonstrates that when a spell misses, it is usually because the magical practitioner's goal wasn't clear enough at the onset. Be certain of your goals and precise with your intent. The result of your magical efforts will astound you.

Once the base is solidly cast, the magical weaving commences. As you knit, keep in mind that the purled stitches belong to the Lord and the knitted stitches belong to the Lady. Feel the balance of the stitches and of the needles, and the harmony they project. Experience the connective process fully as one stitch loops into another. Become the fabric and let the fabric become you.

When you have gotten in tune with the project (this might take a few rows), focus fully on the intended result. Visualize exactly how things will take place and how your goal will materialize. Play the scenario over and over in your mind as you work on the project, willing it to happen just as you plan. When the scenario is firmly fixed in your mind, chant words relevant to the project outcome. Chanting rhythmically with the movement of the needles will help to keep your focus.

For example, if you were knitting something to bring love into your life, you might chant something like:

Bring a perfect love to me
Make him all that he should be
This perfect love shall harm no one
Now as I will, so be it done!

Though it takes concentration and determined focus, getting results with magical needlecraft is not difficult. Just remember that you are the catalyst and you are responsible for the magical energies that you set into motion. Build a solid base, and the results will surpass your wildest dreams.

Nine-Square Log Cabin Meditation Mat

Project design by Dorothy Morrison.

This meditation mat is not only beautiful and easy to knit, but it also makes an excellent addition to your magical tool supply. Because meditation is a balancing tool, use the magically symmetrical garter stitch in knitting this project. Work it one square at a time with a total of nine squares, arranged in three rows of three. To further the magical balance, I suggest working it in dark and light colors.

As you work this project, remember to concentrate on balance, open mindedness, and foresight.

Materials

size 10 knitting needles

8 ounces knitting worsted (color A)

4 ounces knitting worsted (color B)

4 ounces knitting worsted (color C)

4 ounces knitting worsted (color D)

4 ounces knitting worsted (color E)

Note

Knit the entire project using two strands of yarn as one. Because of the constant color changes, it is important to work the log cabin pattern by winding small balls of color for use before beginning. Using the smaller balls prevents yarn from being "carried" across the back of the work; this makes the mat reversible. Make 4 balls of A and 2 of each other color.

To Make the Mediation Mat

Row 1. Using two strands of yarn as one, with color A cast on 30 sts; knit.

Row 2. Knit.

Row 3. Knit.

Row 4. Knit.

Row 5. With color A, k 2 and drop A to the back, k 5 with color E and drop E to the back, knit 5 with color D and drop D to the back, k 16 with color B and drop B to the back, with color A, k 2.

Row 6. Working with all balls of color in the front and taking them to the back when stitches are completed, k 2 with A, k 16 with B, k 5 with D, k 5 with E, k 2 with A.

Rows 7 through 60. Working in the same manner as before, follow the charted color graph (Figure K-1) to the end. Each square represents a stitch.

Sew or crochet the squares together, then empower the mat with this chant:

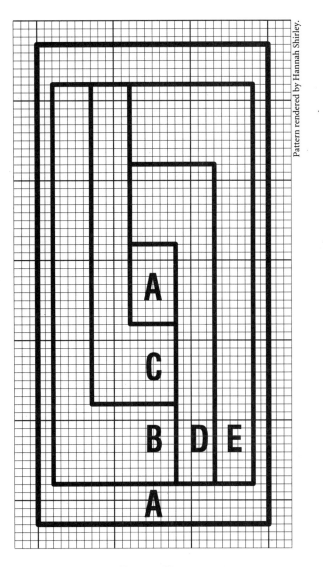

Pattern rendered by Hannah Shirley.

Figure K-1.

Oh little mat of fiber taut:
Bring the balance which I've sought!
Bring symmetry unto my mind,
Relaxing me with your design!
Oh meditation mat of thread:
Ease my mind and clear my head
So that the visions I will view
Come back to me when we are through!

Knitted Bookmark

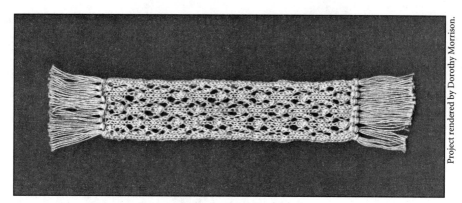

Project rendered by Dorothy Morrison.

Project design by Dorothy Morrison.

Knit this gorgeous bookmark in florette pattern. (See the pages 143 to 144 for instructions.) Though sacred to the Goddess, the airy and lacy eyelets also make it a good prospect for invoking the qualities of Air.

Materials

    size 2 knitting needles

    small ball of crochet thread

    size 4 crochet hook

To Make the Knitted Bookmark

To begin, cast on 17 stitches, then follow the pattern instructions found on pages 143 and 144. Continue to repeat the rows until the piece reaches 7 inches in length, ending on a purl row.

Fringe

Cut 54 four-inch strands of thread and separate them into groups of three. Fold a group in half and centering it, pull it up into a loop with the crochet hook through the last row of stitches and draw the ends through snugly. Repeat the process, distributing the tassels evenly until there are nine tassels on each end.

Enchant the bookmark by chanting:

Oh woven piece of thread and skill!
Mark my place and please instill
The knowledge that has passed my view
Into my mind—quite clear and true!

Rune Bag

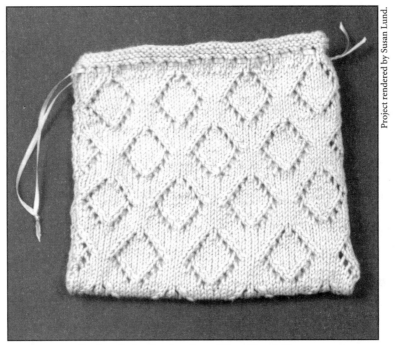

Project rendered by Susan Lund.

Project design by Aaydan of Fort Hood, Texas.

The diamond eyelet stitch used for this bag is appropriate for any type of divination. It suggests the stable and perpetual flow of the Universal energy that surrounds us, and the journey we each take on our personal paths of life. As you knit this project, concentrate on the smooth continuity of your divination readings and meditate upon Odin, the wondrous God who brought us the Runic teachings.

This bag may be constructed of any size, but to enlarge it, a multiple of 12 extra stitches must be added.

Materials

size 2 knitting needles

1–3 balls No. 5 crochet cotton or baby yarn

cotton fabric remnant for lining (optional)

½ yard ⅛" ribbon

matching sewing thread

needle

To Make the Rune Bag

Diamond Eyelet Stitch

(Rows 1 to 28 establish the pattern)

Row 1. K 4, *k 2 tog, yo, k 1, yo, sl 1, k 1, psso, k 7; repeat from * to last 9 sts, k 2 tog, yo, k 1, yo, sl 1, k 1, psso, k 4.

Row 2 AND ALL EVEN ROWS. Purl across.

Row 3. K 3, *k 2 tog, yo, k 3, yo, sl 1, k 1, psso, k 5; repeat from * to last 10 sts, k 2 tog, yo, k 3, yo, sl 1, k 1, psso, k 3.

Row 5. K 2, *k 2 tog, yo, k 5, yo, sl 1, k 1, psso, k 3; repeat from * to last 11 sts, k 2 tog, yo, k 5, yo, sl 1, k 1, psso, k 2.

Row 7. K 1, *k 2 tog, yo, k 7, yo, sl 1, k 1, psso, k 1; repeat from * to last 12 sts, k 2 tog, yo, k 7, yo, sl 1, k 1, psso, k 1.

Row 9. K 3, *yo, sl 1, k 1, psso, k 3, k 2 tog, yo, k 5; re- peat from * to last 10 sts, yo, sl 1, k 1, psso, k 3, k 2 tog, yo, k 3.

Row 11. K 4, *yo, sl 1, k 1, psso, k 1, k 2 tog, yo, k 7; repeat from * to last 9 sts, yo, sl 1, k 1, psso, k 1, k 2 tog, yo, k 4.

Row 13. K 5, *yo, sl 1, k 2 tog, psso, yo k 9; repeat from * across.

Row 15. K 1, yo, sl 1, k 1, psso, *k 7, k 2 tog, yo, k 1, yo, sl 1, k 1, psso; repeat from * to last 10 sts, k 7, k 2 tog, yo, k 1.

Row 17. K 2, yo, sl 1, k 1, psso, *k 5, k 2 tog, yo, k 3, yo, sl 1, k 1, psso; repeat from * to last 9 sts, k 5, k 2 tog, yo, k 2.

Row 19. K 3, yo, sl 1, k 1, psso, *k 3, k 2 tog, yo, k 5, yo, sl 1, k 1, psso; repeat to last 8 sts, k 3, k 2 tog, yo, k 3.

Row 21. K 4, yo, sl 1, k 1, psso, *k 1, k 2 tog, yo, k 7, yo, sl 1, k 1, psso; repeat from * to last 7 sts, k 1, k 2 tog, yo, k 4.

Row 23. K 2, k 2 tog, yo, *k 5, yo, sl 1, k 1, psso, k 3, k 2 tog, yo; repeat from * to last 9 sts, k 5, yo, sl 1, k 1, psso, k 2.

Row 25. K 1, k 2 tog, yo, *k7, yo, sl 1, k 1, psso, k 1, k 2 tog, yo; repeat from * to last 10 sts, k 7, yo, sl 1, k 1, psso, k 1.

Row 27. K 2 tog, yo, *k 9, yo, sl 1, k 2 tog, psso, yo; repeat from * to last 11 sts, k 9, yo, sl 1, k 1, psso.

Row 28. Purl across.

Knitting the Bag

To begin knitting the rune bag, cast on 48 stitches loosely. (Cast on 60 stitches for a medium-size bag or 72 for a larger one.)

Row 1 THROUGH 4. Knit across to end.

Row 5. (Eyelet Row) K2, *yo, k 2 tog; repeat from * across to last 2 sts, k 2.

Row 6. Purl across to end.

Row 7. Knit across to end, increasing 1 st at end of row (49, 61, 73 sts).

Row 8. Purl across to end.

Row 9. Begin the diamond eyelet stitch as outlined above. Work in pattern until total length is almost double the desired length of the bag. End by working a purl row.

NEXT ROW. Knit across to end, decrease 1 st st end of row. (48, 60, 72 sts)

NEXT ROW. Purl across to end.

Next row (eyelet row). K 2, *yo, k 2 tog; repeat from * across to last 2 sts, k 2.

Last four rows. Knit across to end; bind off loosely.

Fold the bag in half, making sure to line up the eyelet row, and carefully sew the side seams. If you prefer to leave the bag unlined, weave the ribbon carefully through the eyelet row and close with a bow.

Lining

Measure the finished bag lengthwise from just below the eyelet row. Double this figure and add a ⅝-inch seam allowance for the fabric length. Measure the bag width and add the same seam allowance to both sides (1¼ inch). Fold the fabric in half and iron carefully.

Sew both side seams with a ⅝-inch seam, then press them open. Fold the top edge over ⅝ inch and sew, being certain to keep side seams flat. Keeping raw edges together, put the lining inside the bag and carefully tack it just below the eyelet row. Weave the ribbon through the eyelet row and secure it with a bow.

To enchant your new rune bag, use the chant suggested for the Crocheted Tarot Bag in the project section of Chapter Five, but substitute Odin for Ashtaroth.

Magical Multi-purpose Muffler

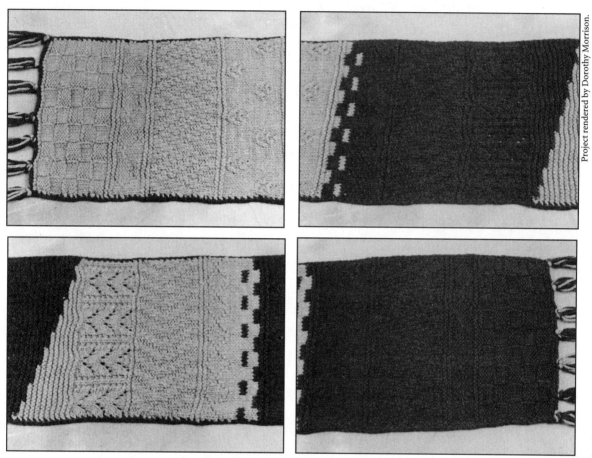

Project rendered by Dorothy Morrison.

Project design by Dorothy Morrison.

Celebrate the Elements, the Lord and Lady, and Their abundance by knitting this beautiful scarf. Blocks of palm fronds and baby ferns represent the Lord and Lady, respectively, while butterfly, candle stitch, ribbed chevron, and block stitches signify Air, Fire, Water, and Earth. The quilted diamonds pattern symbolizes prosperity, fertility, and fruition.

This muffler also boasts the protective bonus of tassels. For centuries, occult practitioners have revered the tassel as a safeguard against evil, aggravation, and psychic devilment. Use seven tassels on each end of the scarf to minimize repetition of your karmic lessons.

Materials

size 8 knitting needles

2 skeins knitting worsted

crochet hook (for attaching tassels)

Additional Abbreviations

C2RK K front of second st on left needle, but not passing st off; k the skipped st, then drop both sts onto the right needle.

C2LK K back of second st on left needle, but not passing st off; k back of skipped st, then drop both sts on to the right needle.

Stitches Used in the Muffler

Quilted Diamonds

Row 1. *K 9, p 1*.

Rows 2 AND 8. K 2, *p 7, k 3*, p 7, k 1.

Rows 3 AND 7. P 2, *k 5, p 5*, k 5, p 3.

Rows 4 AND 6. K 4, *p 3, k 7*, p 3, k 3.

Row 5. P4, *k 1, p 9*, k 1, p 5.

Ribbed Chevron

Row 1. *P 2, k 2, p 2, k 1, p 2, k 2, p 1*.

ALL EVEN ROWS. Knit the purl sts and purl the knit sts of the previous row.

Row 3. *P 1, k 2, p 2, k 3, p 2, k 2*.

Row 5. *K 2, p 2, k 2, p 1, k 2, p 2, k 1*.

Row 7. *K 1, p 2, k 2, p 3, k 2, p 2*.

Palm Fronds

Rows 1 AND 5. K 6, *k 2, c2rk, c2lk, k 8*.

ALL EVEN ROWS. Purl across.

Row 3. K 6, *k 1, c2rk, k 2, c2lk, k 7*.

Row 7. K 6, *k 3, sl 1, k 1, psso and knit it before dropping off needle, k 9*.

Row 9. Knit across.

Rows 11 AND 15. *k 1, c2rk, c2lk, k 10*, c2rk, c2lk, k 1.

Row 13. *c2rk, k 2, c2lk, k 8*, c2rk, k 2, c2lk.

Row 17. K 2, *sl 1, k 1, psso and knit, k 12*, sl 1, k 1, psso and knit, k 2.

Row 19. Knit across.

Butterfly

Rows 1 AND 3. K 5, *k 2 tog, yo, k 1, yo, sl 1, k 1, psso, k 5*.

Rows 2 AND 4. *P 7, sl 1 p-wise, p 2*, p 5.

Rows 5 AND 11. Knit across.

Rows 6 AND 12. Purl across.

Rows 7 AND 9. *K 2 tog, yo, k 1, yo, sl 1, k 1, psso, k 5*, k 2 tog, yo, k 1, yo, sl 1, k 1, psso.

Rows 8 AND 10. *P 2, sl 1 p-wise, p 7*, p 2, sl 1 p-wise, p 2.

Baby Ferns

Row 1 AND ALL ODD ROWS. Purl across.

Row 2. *K 2 tog, k 2, yo, k 1, yo, k 2, sl 1, k 1, psso, p 1, k 1, p 1*.

Row 4. *K 2 tog, k 1, yo, k 3, yo, k 1, sl 1, k 1, psso, p 1, k 1, p 1*.

Row 6. *K 2 tog, yo, k 5, yo, sl 1, k 1, psso, p 1, k 1, p 1.

To Knit the Muffler

NOTE. Though the instructions do not reflect this, always knit the first and last three stitches of every row.

ROW 1. Begin by casting on 51 sts. Knit across.

ROW 2 THROUGH 3. Knit across.

ROW 4 THROUGH 25. Work in block stitch. (Instructions found on page 147.)

ROW 26 THROUGH 29. Knit across.

ROW 30 THROUGH 39. Work in quilted diamonds stitch. (Instructions found on previous page.)

ROWS 40 THROUGH 43. Knit across.

ROWS 44 THROUGH 63. Work in ribbed chevron stitch. (Instructions found on previous page.)

ROWS 64 THROUGH 67. Knit across.

ROWS 65 THROUGH 83. Work in palm fronds stitch (see instructions on previous page.)

ROWS 84 THROUGH 87. Knit across.

ROWS 88 THROUGH 107. Work in butterfly stitch (see instructions on previous page).

ROWS 108 THROUGH 111. Knit across.

ROWS 112 THROUGH 131. Work in candle stitch. (Instructions found on page 146.)

ROWS 132 THROUGH 135. Knit across.

ROWS 136 THROUGH 155. Work in baby ferns stitch. (Instructions found on previous page.)

ROWS 156 THROUGH 168. Knit across.

ROWS 169 TO END. Work the previous patterns for the recommended number of rows in reverse order, beginning with baby ferns and ending with block stitches; then knit three rows and bind off.

Tassels

Cut yarn into 17-inch lengths, using six pieces for each tassel. To attach the tassels, gather six strands and fold them in half forming a loop. Draw the loop up through a stitch (a crochet hook is handy for this process), pass the ends through the loop, and pull tightly. Evenly space seven tassels on each end of the scarf.

Magical Shawl

Project rendered by Susan Lund.

Project design by Elayne of Wichita, Kansas.

This beautiful shawl is so simple to knit that even the beginner can be assured of success. Worked in garter stitch—the stitch of magical balance—this project may be magically imbued with several spells during the fringing process.

Materials

size 11 knitting needles

8 ounces knitting worsted

large-eyed tapestry needle

To Knit the Shawl

ROW 1. Cast on 236 sts loosely; knit across.

ROW 2. K 3, k 2 tog, k 111, k 2 tog, put and keep a marker on needle, sl 1 knit-wise, k 1, psso, k 111, sl 1 knit-wise, k 1, psso, k 3. (4 sts decreased)

ROW 3. Knit across.

ROW 4. K 3, k 2 tog, knit to within 2 sts of marker, k 2 tog, sl marker, sl 1 knit-wise, k 1, psso, k to within last 5 sts, sl 1 knit-wise, k 1, psso, k 3. (4 sts decreased)

Repeat Rows 3 and 4 until only 12 sts remain, then knit one row.

NEXT ROW. K 4, k 4 tog, k 4. (9 sts remaining)

FOLLOWING ROW. Knit across.

FINAL ROW. K 3 tog three times. Break yarn leaving a 10" length. Thread length into tapestry needle and draw the remaining sts together, fastening them securely.

Fringe

Cut yarn into 16-inch lengths. Following the procedure for tassels outlined in the Magical Muffler (page 158), knot one length in every stitch along the outside edges.

As you tie the fringe to the shawl, concentrate on the purpose for enchantment and try this knot magic spell. You may, if you wish, enchant the shawl for several purposes, using nine pieces of fringe for each magical objective. To begin the spell, chant one line while knotting each strand of yarn:

By knot of ONE, the spell's begun
By knot of TWO, it cometh true
By knot of THREE, so mote it be
By knot of FOUR, this power I store
By knot of FIVE, the spell's alive
By knot of SIX, this spell I fix
By knot of SEVEN, events I'll leaven
By knot of EIGHT, it will be fate
By knot of NINE, what's won is mine.

Stockinette Stitch Cape
(with Crocheted Border)

Project rendered by Marcia Herbster and Mary Lou Rost.

Project design by Dorothy Morrison.

This beautiful cape is a "one-size-fits-all" project and measures six yards across the bottom edge. Because it is worked in stockinette stitch and represents the perfect harmony of the Child, use this cape as a balancer to bring your life back into symmetry. Because the crocheted border has the magical implications of the birth-death-rebirth cycle, this cape can also be used in rituals to invoke the Crone, Her wisdom, and the Mysteries.

Materials

- size 10½ 29" long circular knitting needle
- 36 ounces knitting worsted
- size H crochet hook
- needle markers
- frog closure

To Make the Cape

Row 1. Cast on 54 sts to begin at the neck edge. K 3, yo, k 11*, place a marker on the needle, yo, k 13, repeat from * one time, place a marker on the needle, yo k remaining 14 sts.

Row 2. P 3, yo, *p to marker, sl marker, yo, repeat from * twice, then p to end of row. Repeat Row 2 (knitting on odd rows and purling on even rows) until there are 578 sts on the needle. Bind off loosely, but do not fasten off, slipping the remaining stitch onto the crochet hook.

Crocheted Border

Row 1. Ch 5, turn, sk first st, sc in next st, *ch 5, sk next 2 sts, sc in the next st, repeat from * across (193 loops). Ch 6 and turn.

Row 2. Sc in first loop, *ch 6, sc in next loop, repeat from * across; ch 6 and turn.

Row 3. Repeat Row 2; ch 7 and turn.

Rows 4 AND 5. Repeat Row 2, using a ch 7 in all loops.

Rows 6 AND 7. Repeat Row 2, using a ch 8 in all loops.

Rows 8 AND 9. Repeat Row 2, using a ch 9 in all loops; fasten off.

Fringe (Optional)

As noted in the Magical Muffler project, tasseled fringes increase the power of any needlework project. Thus, you may choose to add a fringe to the border of this cape.

Cut yarn into 16-inch pieces. Working with groups of four, fold a group of strands in half to form a loop. Draw the strand loop through a crocheted loop, then pull the ends through, making a firm knot. Trim the fringe evenly.

Secure the frog closure to the neck edge. To enchant the cape, bless it with the Elements and say:

Cape of fiber and woven thread:
Add perfect balance to my life
Bring harmony into it, too,
And lead me far away from strife!

Lacy Leaf Edging

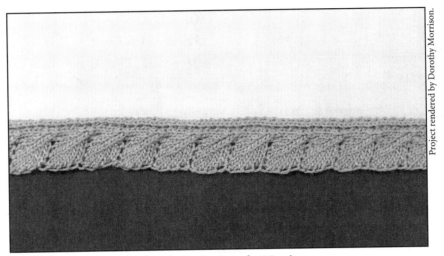

Project rendered by Dorothy Morrison.

Project design by Dorothy Morrison.

This gorgeous edging forms a dainty row of leaves and is the perfect touch for bedroom linens. Because it promotes a fertile, loving vibration, add it to pillowcases, sheets, and accessories to give to a young woman celebrating her first menses or to a newly handfasted couple for their new home. To promote fertile ideas and free-flowing inspriation, add it to a table runner that sits under your computer or other work surface.

Materials

size 1 knitting needles

crochet thread

To Knit the Lacy Leaf Edging

Row 1. Cast on 12 sts; yo, k 1, yo, k 2, k 2 tog twice, k 2, yo, k 2 tog, k 1.

Row 2 AND ALL EVEN ROWS. Purl across.

Row 3. Yo, k 3, yo, k 1, k 2 tog twice, k 1, yo, k2 tog, k 1.

Row 5. Yo, k 5, yo, k 2 tog twice, yo k 2 tog, k 1.

Row 7. Yo, k 3, k 2 tog, k 2 (yo, k 2 tog) two times, k 1.

Repeat these rows for pattern of desired length, making sure that you end with a purl row before binding off.

Enchant the edging by blessing it with the Elements and saying:

Leaves so fertile, leaves so lush!
Enrich our happiness and love!
Bring fertility to our lives,
And the smile of the Ancients far above!

Suggested Sources for Specialty Knitting Supplies

Lanas Margarita, Inc.
P.O. Box R
Island Heights, NJ 08732
(201) 929-3232

(Write for current price list.)

The Mariposa Tree, Inc.
P.O. Box 040336
Staten Island, NY 10304-0006

(Send $1.50 for current catalogue.)

Mary Lue's Knitting World
101 W. Broadway
St. Peter, MN 56082
(507) 931-3702 ext. 30

(Send $2 for current catalogue and yarn samples.)

Patternworks, Inc.
P.O. Box 1690
Poughkeepsie, NY 12601
(914) 454-5648

(Write for free catalogue.)

The Sensuous Fiber
P.O. Box 44, Parkville Station
Brooklyn, NY 11204
(718) 236-4562

(Send $2 for current catalogue.)

The Silk Tree
Box 78
Whonnock, BC V0M 1S0
Canada
(604) 462-9707

(Send $4 for current catalogue and yarn samples.)

Suggested Sources for Alternative Patterns

Miss Chiff
Misc. by Miss Chiff
10131 East 32nd St., Apt. C
Tulsa, OK 74146-1405

InaRae Ussack
Craft/Crafts Magazine
P.O. Box 441
Ponderay, ID 83852

Suggested Reading List

Barbara Abbey, *The Complete Book of Knitting* (New York: Viking Press, Inc., 1971).

Joan Fisher, *Joan Fisher's Guide to Knitting* (Trewin Copplestone Publishing, Ltd., 1973).

McCall's Big Book of Needlecrafts (ABC Needlework and Crafts Magazines, Inc., 1982). Published in 1989 by Chilton Book Company, Radnor, Penn.; published in 1989 by VNR Publishers, Scarborough, Ontario, Canada.

Mildred Graves Ryan, *The Complete Encyclopedia of Stitchery* (Garden City, N.Y.: Doubleday & Company, Inc., 1979).

Barbara G. Walker, *Sampler Knitting* (New York: Charles Scribner's Sons, 1973).

Magical
Dyeing, Spinning,
and Weaving
The Ancient Arts

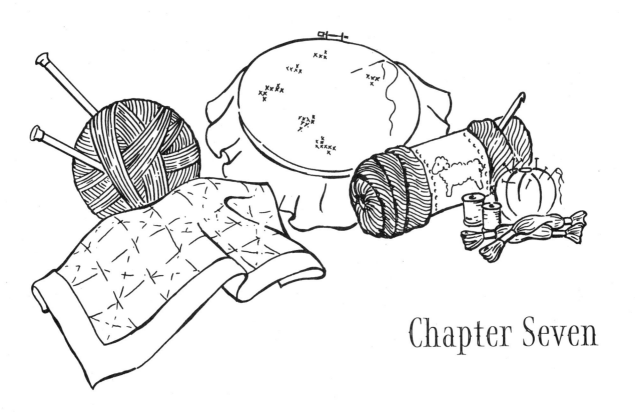

Chapter Seven

Spirit of flax
And cotton plants
Moths long-fled from self-made bed
Fluttering wings echoed
In the needle's flash
Father Sun
Mother Rain
Hands that gathered your bountiful gift
Wove the fibers into thread
And cloth
Hands that spun and dyed the floss
Gather please
To witness and bless
What we have made
Our assembled gifts
And mingled love
Greater than any particular one.
May this tiny part of each of us
Bring beauty into many eyes
Until the time may come
For cloth and silk's return to Earth
and Light.

—Elizabeth J. Campbell

Dyeing: Strolling Across Nature's Rainbow

All color is magical, and those obtained from Mother Nature's rainbow can add a real boost to your projects. Natural dyeing allows the herbs, flowers, bark, and roots used for coloring to add their own magical vibrations to your work. Even better, the dyeing process has its own set of rituals.

In working with plant dyes, try fibers such as cotton, wool, linen, or silk. Most artificial fibers don't absorb dye well and the colors tend to come out spotty and uneven.

Mordanting: Preparing the Fiber for Dye

Before dyeing, wash the fiber at least twice to get rid of any dirt, oil, sizing, and starch. The fiber then undergoes a preparatory process called mordanting. A mordant is a natural or chemical substance that saturates the fiber and seals in the color. Never skip mordanting.

A friend of mine brewed a gorgeous magenta dye from beet juice. It was the perfect shade for a project she had in mind. She worked in the wool, but a putrid shade of brown appeared instead of the rich shade she had envisioned. The problem? No mordant. She didn't realize that wool needed a mordant and assumed that dyeing was a what-you-see-is-what-you-get process. It's not. Almost every fiber needs a mordant to enable it to grab the color in the dyebath.

Alkaline mordants work well for cotton and other plant fibers, while acidic mordants work better on wool, silk, and other animal fibers. Unless your dye recipe reads otherwise, mordant wool with three tablespoons of alum and one tablespoon of cream of tartar. For cotton, use four tablespoons of alum and a tablespoon of washing soda.

To prepare the mordant bath, draw three to four gallons of water for each pound of fiber. This amount of water allows the fiber to move easily through the bath. Dissolve the mordant in the water and bring it to a simmer on the stove. Toss in the fiber and let it simmer for one hour. Chant over the pot several times:

Fiber clean and fiber pure!
Into each thread soak mordant cure
So you will grab the color dye
That I have now in my mind's eye!

Turn off the stove and allow the bath to cool. Remove the fiber and rinse it several times to remove excess mordant.

Soak the fiber in clean water while you prepare the dye bath. This ensures even distribution of color.

Preparing the Dye Bath: The Magic of Color

Prepare a dye bath by cooking plant material for a recommended length of time. Use one to two ounces of plant material to every quart of water. Simmer flowers for fifteen to thirty minutes; cook leaves and stems at medium heat for at least forty-five minutes; boil nutshells, roots, and bark for approximately one hour.

Once the bath reaches the required shade, strain out the plant material and immerse the damp, mordanted fiber in the dye. If necessary, add water to the pot so the material can move freely. Most fibers obtain deep color from a thirty-minute simmer, but allowing the material to cool overnight in the bath makes it more colorfast.

Charm the dye and fiber before you leave it to soak by chanting:

Magical color! Nature's hue!
Infuse this fiber through and through!

Saturate each fiber thoroughly
With magic of flower, leaf, bark, root, and tree!

After you remove the fiber from the dye, let it rest for three or four hours so the dye can settle thoroughly into the fibers. After the allotted time, wash the material thoroughly in warm water with dishwashing liquid, and rinse it repeatedly until the water runs clear. Leave the fiber to dry on wire screens or hang it outside on the clothesline.

There is no end to the plant materials you can use in natural dyeing. Many of these materials probably live in your own backyard. What's more, the same plant combined with different mordants can create a variety of colors, making the dyeing process very inexpensive. (For your convenience, a chart of plants, mordants, and the colors you can produce with them is given on the following page.)

Most of the fun to be had with magical dyeing is in experimentation, so feel free to try different recipes and create your own personal tints and hues. Allow each step of the process to become its own individual ritual. The degree to which the combining energies enhance the magical flow is astounding.

Natural Dyes and Mordants

Color	Dyestuff	Mordant
Pink	Red beets	Alum
	Cranberries	Alum
Rose-Red	Cochinea	Alum
Bright red	Cochineal (concentrated)	Tin
Red-Purple	Cochineal	Chrome
Blue-Purple	Cochineal	Iron sulphate
Purple	Logwood chips	Alum
	Concord grapes	Alum
Blue	Indigo	Hydrosulfite
	Fustic chips	Alum
Navy Blue	Logwood chips	Iron sulphate
Green	Bracken fern	Blue vitriol
	Grass	Blue vitriol
	Lily-of-the-Valley leaves	Alum
Olive Green	Moss	Iron sulphate
	Onion skins (dried)	Iron sulphate
Light Olive	Green lichens	Alum
Yellow	White birch leaves	Alum
	Goldenrod blossoms	Alum
	Milkweed blossoms	Alum
	Peach leaves	Alum
Light Gold	Marigold blossoms	Alum
Deep Gold	Marigold blossoms	Chrome
Bright Gold	Onion skins (dried)	Chrome
Shrimp	Tea	Alum
Orange	Onion skins (dried)	None
	Madder	Tin
	Lichens	Tin
Orange-Red	Madder	Alum
Brown	Red Sandalwood	Alum
	Cutch	Alum
	Henna	Alum or iron
	Horse chestnut	Alum
Light Brown	Coffee	Alum
Tan	Birch bark	Alum
	Maple bark	Alum
	Sumac berries	Alum
Gray-Black	Walnut hulls	Iron sulphate
	Maple bark	Iron sulphate
	Sumac berries	Iron sulphate
Black	Logwood chips (concentrated)	Iron sulphate

Suggested Sources for Dye Plants and Seeds

The Flowery Branch
P.O. Box 1330-HCD
Flowery Branch, GA 30542

(Send $2 for catalogue.)

Goodwin Creek Farms
P. O. Box 83
Williams, OR 97544
(503) 846-7357

(Send $1 for catalogue.)

Renaissance Acres
4450 Valentine Rd.
Whitmore Lake, MI 48189

(Send a self-addressed, stamped envelope for free brochure or $2 for a catalogue.)

The Sandy Mush Herb Nursery
Surrett Cove Road—HBC
Liecester, NC 28748-9622

(Send $4 for catalog; amount is refundable on first order.)

Suggested Sources for Ready-to-Use Natural Dyes and Mordants

Coupeville Spinning and Weaving Shop
P.O. Box 520
Coupeville, WA 98239
(206) 678-4447

(Send $2 for catalog; amount is refundable on first order.)

The Batik and Weaving Supplier
393 Massachussetts Ave.
Arlington, MA 02174
(617) 646-4453

(Send $2 for current catalogue.)

Creek Water Wool Works
P.O. Box 716
Salem, OR 97308
(503) 585-3302

(Send $3 for current catalogue.)

DBP Unlimited
P.O. Box 1344
Duarte, CA 91010
(818) 357-8677

(Write for price list.)

Diana's Designs
7011 Spieth Road
Medina, OH 44256
(216) 722-2021

(Send a self-addressed, stamped envelope for free price list.)

Spinning: The Magic of Humankind

When I was nine, my favorite person was Mrs. Mattern, the keeper of the public library. Travel agent, tour guide, and road crew, she paved the way for those magical journeys into bookland. She recognized my thirst for knowledge and served up an endless supply of books as if they were some sort of divine nectar. I absorbed each one and came back every day begging for more. As if by magic, the librarian always had something new and refreshing waiting for me.

Then one day, there was nothing left to read. Nothing suitable for my age range, anyway. Desolate, I turned to leave. But as if by magic, Mrs. Mattern produced a book for me—a book of Greek mythology.

It was filled with adventures of the gods and goddesses; epics; and tales of suspense, happiness, and tragedy. I still remember in vivid detail the first myth I read. It was the story of the Three Fates, the women who controlled the cycle of life and exercised their power through needlework. Clotho spun the thread of life and initiated the birth process. Lachesis measured the thread against the personal actions, trials, and tribulations of each being while she wound it on life's bobbin. And when the time came, Atropos cut the thread of life, bringing the gift of peace and rest. It was the first time I realized there might be more to needlework than met the eye.

The first American settlers relied heavily upon the spinner's skill, because cloth was scarce and expensive. Laws regulating spinning production were levied to ensure enough thread to clothe the growing population. According to these laws, each family had to spin thirty pounds of thread per year. The penalties for not meeting the quota were stiff, so many families took in unmarried relatives—known as spinsters—to produce the thread for them. The importance of spinsters probably prompted this well known nursery rhyme:

> Cross Patch
> Draw the latch,
> Sit by the fire and spin.
> Take a cup
> And drink it up,
> Then call your neighbors in.

> —Mother Goose

Though we seldom think about how dependent we are on spun fiber, human civilization would never have evolved the way it did without cordage, yarn, and thread.

Thread is just as vital as fiber to our magical existence. It covers us—our altars, our stones, tools, cards, runes, and much more. It is indispensable in preparing herbal infusions, mojo bags, and magical sachets. It is also fundamental to knot magic, wind magic, and, in the case of the Maypole, fertility magic. As magical practitioners, we automatically use thread to bind, seal, connect, and fuse. We don't even think about it. We just do it. Why?

The magic in spun thread lies in the flawless blending of individual fibers into a unity. There is no seam, no obvious connection, no beginning or end. Only one long, single, flexible fiber. The individual fibers are strong together, like the elements in our spiritual lives that make us who we are and bind us to the Earth. Our energies combine to form the thread with which the fabric of the magical realm is woven. Because we are the thread, it is little wonder that we use it so often.

Nearly any fiber can be spun. Flax, cotton, silk, and wool are common selections, but even domestic animal hair works well. The fur of long-haired cats and dogs with heavy undercoats is a perfect consistency for spinning. Some magical practitioners tat or crochet this thread into little bags that hold magical items such as catnip, cat's-eye stones, and cat whiskers, or dogwood, dogbane, and hound's tongue. This a terrific way to include your pet in magical workings and recycle all that loose hair from grooming time.

Because it is easily accessible throughout the world, most of today's spinners work with raw wool fleece. There is more to spinning the fleeces than leaning to use a wheel, though. The fiber isn't difficult to prepare but does require careful handling before being spun. Fiber preparation is a lengthy process and each step provides it own mini-ritual.

Preparing Wool

Obtaining the Fleece

Plenty of excellent shops across the country specialize in spinning needs, and all of them carry raw wool. Some magical practitioners are lucky enough to have their own sheep, so obtaining the wool is only a matter of shearing them. Most spinners don't handle the shearing themselves, but take their sheep to have it done. Though moral support for the animal figures in, the real reason they accompany the sheep is so they can start the magical process at the beginning.

If you're fortunate enough to be a part of this shearing process, visualize the intended magical goal and add a chant while the wool is being shorn. Try something like:

Purest fleece that falls aground!
Be spelled with magic all around—
Within, without, and all about—
Interwoven all throughout!

Cleaning the Fleece

After shearing, clean the wool by picking out the burs, straw, sticks, and leaves. As you clean the fiber, visualize all bits of negativity lifting away from it, chanting as you work:

Stick and straw and leaf and thorn!
Begone from fiber newly shorn!
So purest fleece is left behind,
And purest magic, unmaligned!

When the fleece is free of plant materials, wash it thoroughly. There are several ways to do this, but using the washing machine is probably easiest. (If you choose this method, please follow the instructions below carefully or you could have a real mess on your hands!) Fill the washer with hot—not warm—water, add a pinch of sea salt to bless the wash, then add some shampoo. Because the lanolin content of wool is high, use a shampoo made for oily hair to remove the grease from the fiber. Turn the machine off once it is full, then add the wool. **Do not agitate the fiber!** (Agitating turns the fleece to felt and renders it useless.) Let the wool soak until thoroughly saturated; concentrate on and visualize the magical projects you wish to make with the fiber and visualize the finished product.

Use the spin cycle to remove the excess water. Carefully pull the wool away from the water spigot of the machine and fill the washer again with hot water to rinse out the shampoo. (Don't forget to turn the machine off again before it begins to agitate.) Rinse the wool thoroughly four times with hot water and, as before, remove the excess water with the spin cycle.

Placing the fleece on an old window screen is a good way to dry it, because the fiber lies flat while getting good air circulation. Drying time varies according to climate and weather conditions. If you have a screened-in porch, try drying the fiber there. It takes much longer for wool to dry if you have to use an unventilated area.

Carding the Wool

When the fiber is completely dry, pick through it again to remove any foreign objects missed in the initial cleaning. Afterward, the wool undergoes a procedure called **carding**. This entails brushing small amounts of fleece between two wire brushes to make it smooth, flexible, and easy to work. Proper carding results in tiny rolls called rolags, and it is from these that spinning fiber is born. Because this process can be time-consuming (depending on the amount of wool you card), it lends itself to further visualization and enchantment. Chanting makes the work go faster, so try one of a magical nature such as:

> **Smooth the fiber, cards so stout!**
> **Brush the old and useless out!**
> **Leave only magic here within**
> **The tiny rolags that I'll spin!**

Spinning Thread

Thread may be spun either with the fingers or on a wheel. Though some practitioners use a hand-held spindle and employ the finger method when spinning, most find the wheel more effective because it produces a sturdier yarn or thread. This sturdiness is important because thread tends to stretch during use, and there is nothing more irritating than yarn that tears apart in the middle of a project. While you may be somewhat intimidated by the spinning wheel's complicated appearance, don't let it keep you from trying one. The wheel is nothing more than a large, hand-held spindle turned on its side and rotated mechanically. Once you learn to use one, I doubt that you will ever want to spin by hand again.

Spinning With the Wheel

The best way to learn to spin on a wheel is to work with one. Familiarize yourself with the different parts of the wheel and their functions. Understanding the wheel and its operation is a battle half-won, because once you know how it works, the thread nearly spins itself.

The first step in spinning is threading the wheel. Tie a few yards of strong hairy yarn to the bobbin; then, guiding it through the tension hooks, turn the wheel slowly while the yarn completes the threading process. Give the wheel a spin in the direction you want it to turn. Although most thread is spun by turning the wheel clockwise to form an S-twist, a very magical thread can be spun by turning the wheel widdershins (counter-clockwise) to form a Z-twist.

Holding the "lead" thread in one hand, loosen some fiber from a rolag and feed it onto the thread with the other hand. As you do this, the fiber will twist itself onto the lead thread and form yarn, then winds itself onto a bobbin or niddy-noddy. If you start to run out of spinning material, add the fiber from another rolag a little at a time and continue the process until the rolags are all gone.

That is all there is to it! Chanting while spinning is a good way to reinforce the magical energy already flowing through the fiber. Try something like the following, or devise a chant of your own.

> Little wheel spin 'round and 'round
> Magical energy, here, abound!
> Enchant this yarn that I now spin—
> Flow through each fiber—thick or thin!

Skeining

After the thread is spun, it must be skeined. The easiest way to handle this is with a little help from a friend. Have someone hold their hands eighteen to twenty-four inches apart while you wind the yarn evenly around them, criss-crossing in the middle to form a figure eight. If no one can help you, try looping it around the top of a ladder-back chair, between two dowels, or even around your feet. Secure the skeins by tying the ends around each loop.

Stretching and Drying

Freshly spun yarn is uneven and elastic. To make it workable, it must undergo a stretching procedure called setting. To set the yarn, immerse the skeins in a tub of very hot water and let them soak until they are thoroughly saturated. Gently squeeze out as much water as you can, then hang the skeins from a ceiling hook. Fold a heavy towel across the base of a coathanger and loop the hook through the bottom of the skein. The weighted coat hanger stretches the yarn, and the towel prevents water from dripping to the floor.

The yarn must be thoroughly dry before use. Depending upon your climate, this may take from two or three days to several weeks. A daily chant during this period adds to the magical capabilities of the yarn. Visualize the air drying the fibers while imbuing them with magical energy and chant something like:

> Air flow in! Air flow out!
> Air flow under, over, around, and about!
> Imbue this fiber with Your energies!
> As I will, so mote it be!

Because yarns and threads are the basis for every magical needlecraft project, learning the art of spinning is well worth the effort. Spinning allows the magical needlecrafter an opportunity to see the creative process through from start to finish, and it lends itself more to magical ritual than any other threadwork I know.

Suggested Sources
for Spinning Supplies

Bear Trap Fibers
Route 2, Box 110A
Ashland, WI 54806
(715) 682-5937

(Write for free price list.)

Clemes & Clemes, Inc.
650 San Pablo Avenue
Pinole, CA 94564
(415) 724-2036

*(Send for free catalogue or
send $2 for wool samples.)*

The Country Craftsman
P.O. Box 412
Littleton, MA 01640
(508) 486-4053

(Write for free brochure and price list.)

Detta's Spindle
2592 Geggen-Tina Road
Maple Plain, MN 55359
(612) 479-2886

*(Send $1.50 for catalogue. Send a self-
addressed, stamped envelope for custom
spinning information. These folks specialize
in dog and cat hair yarns.)*

Weaving: The Harmony Place

The people of prehistoric times depended upon wild animals to feed and clothe them, so they became a wandering sort who moved seasonally to follow the herds. These people also made a rough type of covering by intertwining twigs, reeds, and rushes. Although this covering was not suitable for clothing, it provided an excellent, sturdy shelters. Before long, they refined the art of weaving and learned to make baskets, floor mats, and other items to make their lives easier. Finally, someone realized that bits of fiber could be twisted to produce thread. Spinning was born and the art of weaving was well on its way.

As with any ancient art, much legend and folklore surrounds weaving. An ancient Greek tale relates how the goddesses of Mount Olympus gathered the clouds surrounding the mountain onto their spindles of ivory and gold. The winds turned the distaffs and spun the thread, and Athena wove it into gossamer cloth to clothe them all. Of course, this legend led to the better known tale of the infamous weaving contest in which a spiteful Athena shifted Arachne's shape forever into that of the spider.

Much later the weaving legend of the Navajo surfaced. According to the tale, Spider Woman taught the Navajo to weave upon a loom of her consort's construction. The cross poles consisted of Earth, the warp sticks of the Sun's rays, the heddles of rock crystal and lightning, and the batten of the Sun's halo. A white shell formed the comb.

Spider Woman taught that the inner form of the loom represented the marriage of Mother Earth and Father Sky; the design formed during the weaving process was the child conceived and born of the marriage. The child/design was an expression of perfect beauty and perfect harmony, and by order of the gods, no negative vibration could enter the weaver's mind or heart while at work in the "harmony place."

Weaving is the intertwining of threads to form fabric. The fixed threads are the warp, and the working thread is the weft. As the weft and warp threads cross and interlace, the web or cloth forms.

The very first form of weaving required only the most basic of tools and looms: the fingers. Finger-weaving, which resembles braiding or plaiting, was the original source of Celtic knotwork. This form of weaving is still popular today and the practitioner can use it to produce purses, afghans, and many other useful items.

Later, weavers discovered that using a stick or shuttle to raise every other warp thread made a tighter fabric, made the stitches even, and caused the work to go more quickly. That discovery brought the invention of the loom. A discussion of the many loom types available today and the methods for weaving on them is beyond the scope of this book. However, making an inexpensive frame loom is easy, and weaving on it is a snap.

Making and Using a Loom

To make the loom, stagger small nails across two ends of a wooden picture frame or canvas stretcher. Tie the warp thread to the first nail at the bottom of the loom and wrap it tautly around the first nail at the top. Bring the thread back around the second nail at the bottom, up to the second nail at the top and so on until the warp threads cover the entire loom. Then tie the thread securely to the last nail on the bottom row.

Weave the weft threads by using a shuttle or by threading the weft thread through a very large plastic needle. Tie the weft thread to the warp thread on the outer right-hand edge of the loom, then weave it in and out through the rest of the warp threads. If the weft is at the bottom of a warp when you reach the left edge, bring it up over the last warp thread and continue by weaving from left to right. If the thread is on top, take it under the last warp thread.

After you finish the last row, tie off the weft thread by attaching it to a warp thread just as you did when you began. Then, using a crochet hook and beginning opposite the dangling end of the tied-off weft, slip the warp threads from the nails one at a time and hook each loop through the loop next to it to form an even edge. Before you slip off the last loop, hook the weft thread through it. Then slip off the last warp loop and weave the weft back through the work to hide and secure it. Repeat the process for the other end of the fabric.

What you can weave with this loom depends on the size of your frame and the scale of your yarn, but some of the most popular projects to loom are potholders, place mats, and tote bags. For magical purposes, Tarot card or rune bags and altar cloths immediately come to mind. Try using crochet cotton or pearl rayon for miniature items such as charm bags and sachets, sport yarns for divination bags and altar cloths, and knitting worsted or rug yarns for heavier items like potholders, placemats, tote bags, and clothing.

Every fabric available on the market today (with the exception of felt) is created by weaving. This art is at the foundation of every form of needlework, whether you knit, crochet, embroider, or sew a magical project. Threads intertwine one with another, thoughts weave together into tangible form, and you sit in the harmony place—forever peaceful, loving, and beauteous.

Suggested Sources for Weaving Supplies

Ayotte's Designery
P.O. Box 287
Center Sandwich, NH 03227
(603) 284-6915
(Send $1 for current catalogue and price list.)

Earth Guild
One Tingle Alley
Asheville, NC 28801
(800) 327-8448
(Send $2 for catalogue; amount refundable on first order.)

Fibre Crafts
38 Center Street
Clinton, NJ 08809
(201) 735-4469
(Write for free brochure and price list.)

Gilmore Looms
1032 N. Broadway
Stockton, CA 95205
(209) 463-1545
(Write for free brochure and price list.)

Grandor Industries Ltd.
716 E. Valley Parkway, Unit 48
Escondido, CA 92025
(619) 743-2345
(Send $5 for current catalogue and yarn samples.)

Suggested Reading List

Pauline Campanelli, *The Wheel of the Year: Living the Magical Life* (Llewellyn Publications, St. Paul, Minn., 1988).

Bette Hochberg, *Spin Span Spun* (Bette Hochberg and Bernard Hochberg, Berkeley, Calif., 1979).

Virginia G. Hower, *Weaving, Spinning, and Dyeing: A Beginner's Manual* (Prentice-Hall, Englewood Cliffs, N.J., 1976).

Eunice Svinicki, *Step-by-Step Spinning* (Western Publishing Company, Inc., Racine, Wis., 1974).

Nell Znamierowski, *Step by Step Weaving* (Western Publishing Company, Inc., Racine, Wis., 1967; published by Golden Press, Inc., New York).

Magical
Afterthoughts

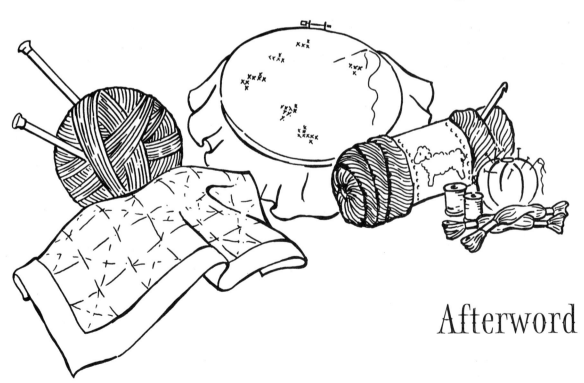

Afterword

Needlework:
The Health Enhancer

The mind is a powerful tool that can work for us or against us. A friend of mine learned this firsthand when she took a position in the dog-eat-dog world of commissioned sales. Because her livelihood depended upon the amount of merchandise she sold, she quickly learned that the power of suggestion played a large part in her financial success. While she knew the merchandise and its greatest selling points, she simply could not outdo her co-worker Tom when it came to moving inventory.

A basic exercise of the mind worked wonders for her, though. The trick was to ask Tom whether he was feeling all right. Within minutes, his mind would tell his body it wasn't feeling well, and he would go home for the day. His brain was working against him.

The brain can work for us, too. Programmed properly, this powerful tool can speed healing to our bodies and adjust our general mindset.

My interest in the healing properties of needlecraft was piqued when a fellow practitioner shared some research findings with me. She discovered that most people who easily tap into their spiritual selves do so while focused on a craft project of some sort. This makes sense because a mind intently focused on something tends to fall into a naturally induced trance. People in this state get more in touch with the inner self than they can through conscious thought, and this makes it possible to get to the bottom of most problems that plague the mind or body.

During her investigation, the practitioner found a therapist who encourages patients to bring needlework with them to sessions. He describes it as "natural therapy" and much prefers it to hypnosis or confrontation therapy, which sometimes shocks the patient into physical symptoms or causes them to hide from their real fears.

Although I have always enjoyed working with all forms of needlecraft, I never made the connection between my general good health and my relish for challenging arts and crafts projects. As I talked to others about the subject matter of this book, I found a number of them use needlework as a means of healing. I delved more deeply into the possibilities, discussing them with physicians, therapists, and medical personnel. The conversations were enlightening and helped to change my perspective on the magical qualities of needle arts.

Needlecraft is not a strenuous physical exercise, and working with it allows the body to relax. The body heals best during relaxed periods, because physical inertia must be present for cells to regenerate. Mild trance or a meditative condition is precisely the state of mind achieved when working with all types of needlework. Perhaps that is why occupational therapists find needlecraft so beneficial to their patients. Not only do simple projects ease the mind and relax the body, they increase dexterity in those who have trouble with eye-to-hand coordination.

Needlework is a terrific prescription for people with a mental illness or those who are dealing with stress and depression. Many needle arts are very soothing. In the rhythmic motion of cross stitching, for example, the patterns of the mind fall into regularity and harmony eventually prevails over cacophony. In needlework, the hand taps out the rhythm the mind must follow. Because the mind must pay close attention to the work at hand, it is unable to wander aimlessly toward grief and depression. An occupied mind allows the person to deal with problems in a timely fashion, rather than becoming totally overwhelmed by them.

The next time you are down in the dumps or have to stay in bed with the flu, give needlework a shot. Though its rehabilitative powers won't replace the help of your physician, you will feel better and recuperate quickly.

Magical Ethics and Personal Responsibility

Needles and Threads and Fabrics and Floss,
Weave tightly the Magic of firmly spun
spells—
But the ethical thought behind the rite,
Only the Three-fold Law shall tell!

—Kalioppe

All of us go through periods where we, at least fleetingly, think of doing something that we might consider unethical. Please remember that all magic is powerful and none should ever be taken lightly. Normally, magic is only as potent as what you put into it, but even desires only haphazardly tossed into the Universe do manifest upon occasion.

For that reason, I urge you to be careful of your wishes and make preparation to accept total responsibility for them, for like the Lord and Lady, the Three-fold Law is ever-present, ever-watchful, and ever-knowing.

Magical
Accouterments
Enhancing the Magic

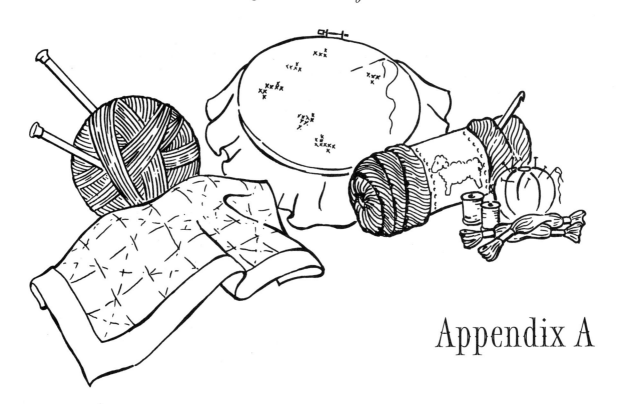

Appendix A

Since there are as many reasons for performing magic as there are precitioners, this appendix has been added for your convenience. Use the patterns here to personalize your projects, strengthen your focus, and carry your messages to the Universe.

Because many of the symbols have rounded shapes, their designs have been charted for backstitch (straight stitch) rather than cross stitch. This alleviates the need for quarter and half stitches to obtain the proper shape. The Elder Futhark runes are the exception; both cross-stitch and backstitch patterns for the runes have been provided.

Modified Theban Alphabet

For many years, the Theban Alphabet, commonly known as the Witches' Alphabet, presented usage problems because it did not hold all the letters we need to form words. InaRae Ussack of *Craft/Crafts Magazine* modified it to contain twenty-six magical letters and devised a simple backstitch form suitable for a variety of uses.

Use it in magical samplers, name plates for your desk, altar cloths, covers for your Book of Shadows—even for your coffee mug (see the Pentagram Coffee Mug project in Chapter Five.)

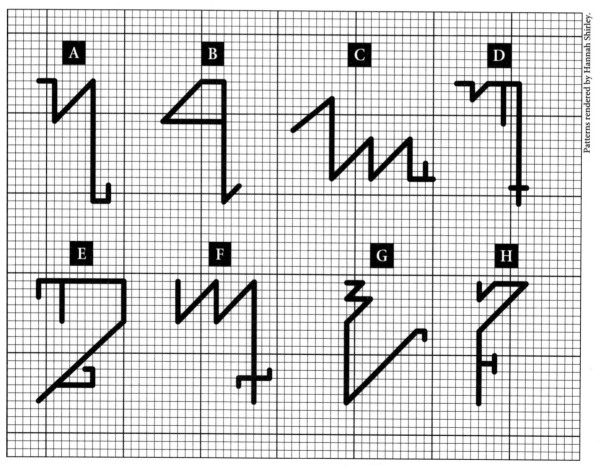

Patterns rendered by Hannah Shirley.

Modified Theban alphabet backstitch patterns.
(Continued on following page.)

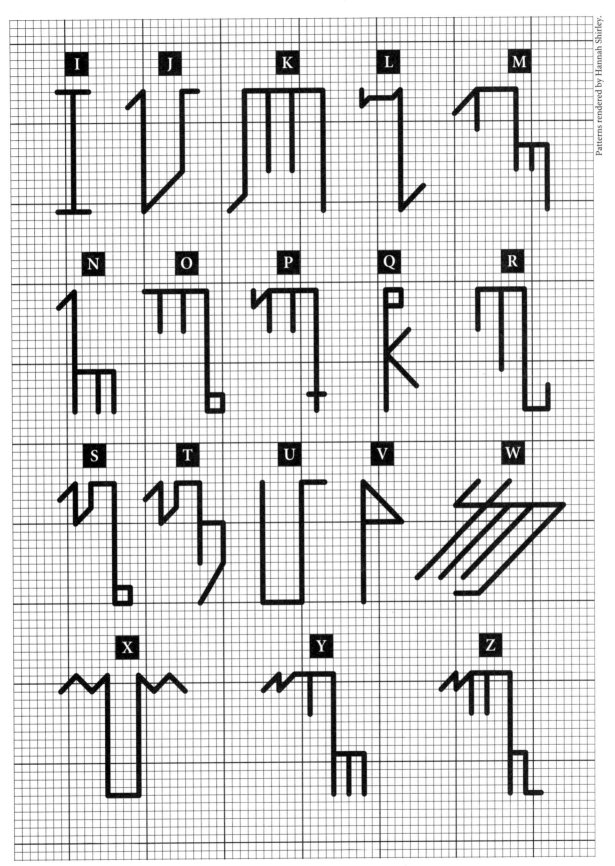

Modified Theban alphabet backstitch patterns.

(Continued from previous page.)

Planetary Symbols

Imbue your needlework projects with specific magical energies by including planetary symbols. This list will help you choose the right planet and symbol for your goals.

SUN. Success, joy, friendship, men's rites, prosperity, business ventures, good health, physical energy, the God.

MOON. Magic, romance, wishes, women's rites, divination, family, home and hearth, medicine, gardening, the Goddess.

MERCURY. Communication, inspiration, study, learning, teaching, self-improvement, comprehension.

VENUS. Art, music, pleasure, entertainment, love, romance, luxury.

MARS. Surgical procedures, politics, hunting, sports, physical endurance, competitive ventures.

JUPITER. Material gain, prosperity, luck, gambling, accomplishment, success, legal problems.

SATURN. Karmic lessons, reincarnation, the mysteries, wisdom, death, disease, the elderly.

URANUS. Imagination, opinions and debates, self-confidence.

NEPTUNE. Clairvoyance, prophecy, divination, magic.

PLUTO. Spiritual issues, soul searching, connection to the Divine Self, guidance.

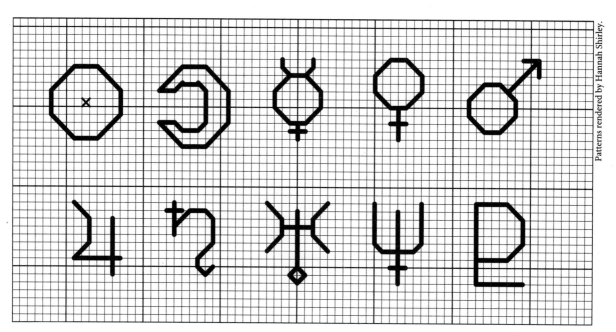

Patterns rendered by Hannah Shirley.

Planetary symbols backstitch patterns.

Astrological Symbols

These astrological symbols really need no explanation. Use them to personalize projects for yourself or someone else.

For instance, you can make the poppet described in Chapter Two look like a specific person by choosing hair and eye colors, but stitching the person's astrological sign on the poppet tells the Universe about his or her personality. You could also stitch the astrological symbol of the person you love on the Loving Dream Pillow (see Chapter Four) or mark the spine of your Enchanted Notebook or Book of Shadows Cover (see Chapter Three) with your own astrological sign. Because the patterns use backstitches, these astrological symbols can easily be applied to magical sewing and patchwork projects as well as embroidery projects.

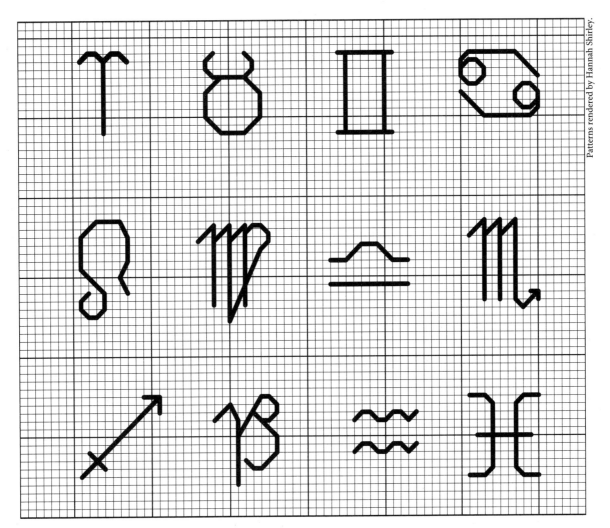

Patterns rendered by Hannah Shirley.

Astrological symbols backstitch patterns.

Elder Futhark Runes

Incorporating the power of the runes into your needlework project tells the Universe what you want to accomplish with your magic. The cross-stitch patterns given on the opposite page can be used in just about any embroidery project, but specifically for the Runic Pin or Pendant project described in Chapter Four. The backstitch versions on page 190 can be stitched onto any project, from emroidery to patchwork to sewing.

Feoh. Success, accomplishment, gain.

Ur. Strength, growth, metamorphosis, passage.

Thorn. Defense, preparedness, passage.

Ansur. Communication; absorption and release of ideas, information, and knowledge.

Rad. Travel, spontaneity, adventure, flexibility.

Ken. Creativity, inspiration, the Muses, arts, crafts, construction.

Geofu. Union, partnership, marriage, strength in numbers.

Wynn. Fulfillment, wishes granted, desires obtained, goals accomplished.

Hagall. Chaos, change, order from confusion.

Nied. Tenacity, stability, endurance.

Is. Standstill, checkmate, deadlock.

Jara. Harvest, rewards, gifts, honors.

Yr. Gateway, transition, discovery.

Peorth. Quest, awareness, uncovering the hidden.

Eolh. Protection, defense, bravery.

Sigel. Victory, completeness, fulfillment of cycle.

Tir. Commitment, aggressiveness, strength of will.

Beorc. Birth, conception, manifestation of ideas.

Eoh. Change, growth, flexibility, travel.

Mann. Interaction, friendships, relationships, support network.

Lagu. Intuition, heightened awareness, altered consciousness, magic.

Ing. Transformation, preparation, culmination.

Daeg. Emergence, metamorphosis, growth.

Othel. Ancestory, pastlives, personal history, cultural bonds.

Elder Futhark Runes cross-stitch patterns.

Elder Futhark Runes backstitch patterns.

Cross Stitch Pentagram and Arabic Alphabet

The cross stitch pentagram pattern (below) was the one I used on the Enchanted Notebook or Book of Shadows cover in Chapter Three. It was created by Karen Everson of Moongate Designs, and incorporates two colors of your choice.

The pentagram is perhaps one of the most magically symbolic of all shapes. It represents the macrocosm of humankind, the forces of Nature in conjunction with the mind, and, for Pagans, the direction of the spiritual path.

Patterns for the backstitch Arabic letters used on the spine of the enchanted cover are shown of the following page.

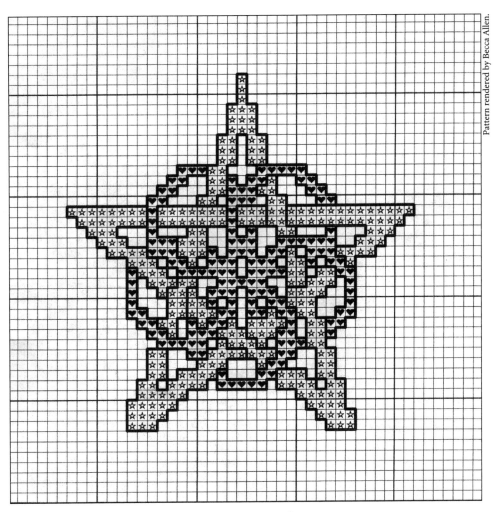

Pattern rendered by Becca Allen.

Pentagram cross stitch pattern.

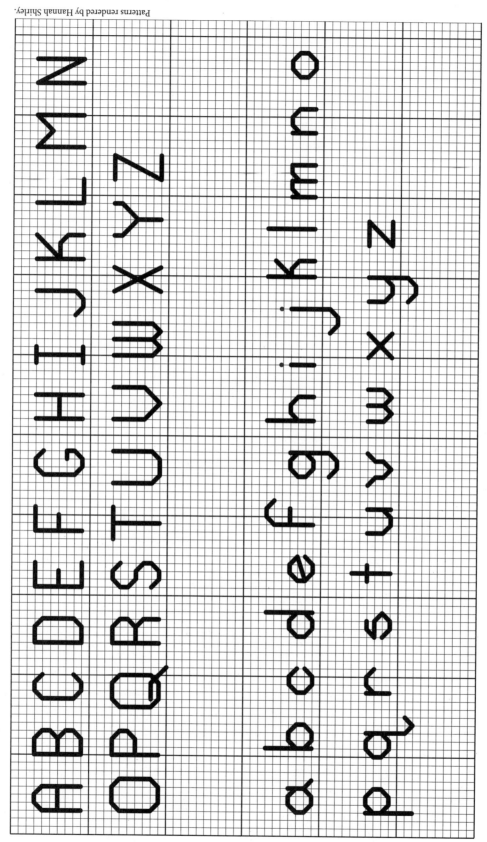

ABCDEFGHIJKLMN
OPQRSTUVWXYZ

abcdefghijklmno
pqrstuvwxyz

Arabic alphabet backstitch patterns.

Magical
Dates and Deities
Celebrating the Magic

Appendix B

Want to enhance magical focus and boost its power? The best way is to find the right deity for the job. Try invoking a deity directly associated with the type of needlework used in your project, then begin work on the project during the deity's feast day or a festival directly related to the needle art of choice.

There are many deities and festival celebrations associated with needlework. Use the tables below to choose the deities and dates that will best suit your purpose.

Dates and Deities Associated With Needlework

	Deity	Special Day
Carding	St. Blaise	
Dyeing	St. Bartholomew	March 4
	St. Helena	August 18
	St. Maurice	February 21
	Iris	
Embroidery	St. Clara of Assisi	November 4
Needles	St. Fiacre of Breuil	August 30
	St. Helena	August 18
	St. Sebastian	February 20
	Kali	
Needlework (general)	Bride or Brigit	Imbolc
	Hestia	
	Vesta	
	Athena	July 10
Scissors	Kali	
	Atropos	

Continued on next page.

	Deity	Special Day
Sewing	St. Bartholomew	March 4
	St. Boniface	June 5
	St. Casimor	March 4
	St. John the Baptist	June 24
	St. Lucy of Syracuse	December 13
Spinning	Clotho	
	Ixchel	
	Arachne	
	Isis	
	St. Catherine *(This day is celebrated in Europe and all spinners take the day off to join in the festivities!)*	November 25
	Spider Woman	
	St. Margaret of Cortona	July 20
Thread	Arachne	
Weaving	Ixchel	
	Athena	July 10
	Arachne	
	St. Blaise	
	St. Lucy of Syracuse	December 13
	St. Bernadino of Siena	May 20
	St. Francis of Assisi	October 4

Festivals Associated With Needlework

Panathenaea (July 10)

A Grecian festival held in honor of Athena, this celebration involves many types of rituals. One of the most interesting is the robe ritual. The statue of Athena is presented with a new robe each year on this day. It is a wonderful day for beginning any magical sewing project.

Feast of the Milky Way (August 9)

According to an ancient Chinese legend, a banished shepherd who had married a weaver crosses the Milky Way each year on this day to visit his wife. This is an excellent day for weaving or magical needlecraft of any type.

Hari No Kuyo: The Festival of Broken Needles (December 2)

This day is celebrated in Japan to honor all women's crafts and tools. Take this opportunity to bless any new additions to your wealth of magical needlecraft supplies.

Day of the Weavers (December 28)

This is the day of a South American festival that honors all weavers. Take the day off and wish upon bits of thread. "Knot" your wish into them and cast the pieces into a blazing fire.

Magical Colors

Another magical needlework power tool is color. It not only mirrors intent, but serves as a constant reminder to the Universe that a spell is ongoing and infinite. Don't worry that the colors you choose for a magical project might clash. Just choose your colors and stick to your decision. Once the project is finished, you will be amazed at its beauty!

Red	Fire, Mother Goddess aspect, vitality, strength, passion, sexual desire, energy.
Pale Blue	Peace, tranquility, protection, good health.
Dark Blue	The Goddess, Water.
Pink	Harmony, romantic love, friendship.
Peach	Kindness, gentleness.
Orange	Attraction.
Yellow	Air, the God, success, joy, creativity.
Green	Earth, growth, fertility, prosperity.
Purple	Akasha, power, spirituality, psychic powers.
White	Maiden Goddess aspect, spiritual guidance; may be substituted for any color, as it is a culmination of all colors in the spectrum.
Black	Crone Goddess aspect, separation, the absence of light.

Guide to Additional Resources

Each of the businesses and individuals listed cheerfully handles mail orders.

Seamstresses, Tailors, and Creators of Magical Clothing

Because we live in a busy world, we often want to make more projects than we have time to manage. If you fall into this category, the following list may help. Each person listed does custom work and is priced reasonably for his or her respective area. Write with your specifications and enclose a self-addressed, stamped envelope for a reply and estimate.

Black Rose Creations
Attn: Sidonya
70 Temple Street
West Boylston, MA 01583

Joyce A. Jordan
501 Kingston Drive
Yukon, OK 73099

Mark Calderwood
10 Essex Street
Bullaburra, NSW 2784
Australia

The Sorcerer's Apprentice
2103 Adderbury Circle
Madison, WI 53711

Creators of Magical Needlecraft Patterns and Designs

A. B. Firethorne Designs
Attention: Aristana
P. O. Box 1414
Guerneville, CA 95446
707/869-9021

(The mainstay of Aristana's Celtic knotwork is worked in leather on hair barrettes. However, custom altar cloths, charm bags, and similar items are available.)

Avalon Oddiments
Attention: Fiona Firefall
P.O. Box 3304
Kansas City, KS 66103

(Hand-sewn dragons, satyrs, mermaids, anatomically correct dolls, and Tarot bags are just a few of the delights available from Avalon Oddiments. Write for a complete list. Custom work is available.)

Incenses, Oils, Stones, and Other General Magical Supplies

Ancient Ways

Attention: Glenn Turner

4075 Telegraph Road

Oakland, CA 94609

(Carries a full line of supplies for the Craft, including books, herbs, oils, incenses, etc. Custom oils and incenses available.)

The Enchanted Apothecary

Attention: Carol

72-01 Austin Street

Forest Hills, NY 11375

1-800-865-5006

(Carries a full line of supplies for the magical practitioner, including Bach flower remedies, herbs and spices, washes, powders, stones, jewelry and music. Truly a one-stop shop!)

Hourglass Creations

Attention: Patricia

492 Breckenridge

Buffalo, NY 14213

(Carries a full line of supplies for the creative Pagan including soaps, lotions, oils, incenses, wands, etc. Custom work available.)

Mountain Rose Herbs

Attention: Julie

P.O. Box 2000

Redway, CA 95560

1-800-879-3337

(This shop specializes in various herbal delights: teas, loose herbs, oils, seeds, books, dream pillows and body care. Custom work available.)

Nature's Treasures

6223 S.E. 15th Street

Midwest City, OK

(Carries full line of occult supplies, incense, oils, herbs, and needlecraft patterns with a Pagan flavor. Custom oils and incenses available.)

Bibliography

Academic American Encyclopedia. Danbury, Conn.: Grolier, Inc., 1985.

Campanelli, Pauline. *The Wheel of the Year: Living the Magical Life*. St. Paul, Minn.: Llewellyn Publications, 1989.

Cunningham, Scott. *Cunningham's Encyclopedia of Magical Herbs*. St. Paul, Minn.: Llewellyn Publications, 1986.

Encyclopedia Americana. Danbury, Conn.: Grolier, Inc., 1989.

Gostelow, Mary, ed. *The Complete Guide to Needlework: Tecniques and Materials*. Secaucus, N.J.: Chartwell Books Inc., 1982 (Quill Publishing Ltd.).

Hangen, Eva C. *Symbols: Our Universal Language*. Wichita, Kan.: McCormick-Armstrong Co., 1962.

Hitchcock, Helyn. *Helping Yourself with Numerology*. West Nyack, N.Y.: Parker Publishing Company, Inc., 1972.

Hochberg, Bette. *Spin Span Spun*. Berkeley, Calif.: Bette Hochberg and Bernard Hochberg, 1979.

Hower, Virginia G. Weaving, *Spinning, and Dyeing: A Beginner's Manual*. Englewood Cliffs, N.J.: Prentice-Hall, 1976.

Johnson, Mary Elizabeth. *Star Quilt*. New York: Clarkson Potter Publishers, 1992.

McCall's Big Book of Needlecrafts. ABC Needlework and Crafts Magazines, Inc., 1982. Published in 1989 by Chilton Book Company, Radnor, Penn.; published in 1989 by VNR Publishers, Scarborough, Ontario, Canada.

McRae, Bobbi. *The Fabric and Fiber Sourcebook*. Newtown, Conn.: The Taunton Press, Inc., 1989.

Medici, Marina. *Good Magic*. New York: Prentice Hall Press, 1988.

Montano, Judith. *Crazy Quilt Odyssey: Adventures in Victorian Needlework*. Lafayette, Calif.: C & T Publishing, 1991.

Myth H. *Runes: Elder Futhark Counted Cross Stitch Patterns & Workbook* (Myth H Magical Needlework Series). Houston, Tex.: Myth H, 1994.

New Book of Knowledge. Danbury, Conn.: Grolier, Inc., 1992.

Pepper, Elizabeth and John Wilcox. *The Witches' Almanac: Complete Astrological Guide Spring 1993 to Spring 1994*. Pentacle Press, Inc., 1993.

Reader's Digest Complete Guide to Needlework. Pleasantville, N.Y.: Reader's Digest Association, Inc., 1979.

Ryan, Mildred Graves. *The Complete Encyclopedia of Stitchery*. Garden City, N.Y.: Doubleday & Company, Inc., 1979.

Skelton, Robin. *Talismanic Magic*. York Beach, Maine: Samuel Weiser, Inc., 1985.

Slater, Herman. *The Magickal Formulary*. New York: Magickal Childe Inc.,1981.

Telesco, Patricia. *Llewellyn's 1994 Magical Almanac*. St. Paul, Minn.: Llewellyn Publications, 1993.

Telesco, Patricia. *The Urban Pagan*. St. Paul, Minn.: Llewellyn Publications, 1993.

Znamierowski, Nell. *Step by Step Weaving*. New York: Golden Press, Inc., 1967. (Western Publishing, Inc.)

——·◄ Index ►·—

- T -

- V -

- W -

- Y -

☾ LOOK FOR THE CRESCENT MOON

Llewellyn publishes hundreds of books on your favorite subjects! To get these exciting books, including the ones on the following pages, check your local bookstore or order them directly from Llewellyn.

ORDER BY PHONE

- Call toll-free within the U.S. and Canada, 1-800-THE MOON
- In Minnesota, call (612) 291-1970
- We accept VISA, MasterCard, and American Express

ORDER BY MAIL

- Send the full price of your order (MN residents add 7% sales tax) in U.S. funds, plus postage & handling to:

  Llewellyn Worldwide
  P.O. Box 64383, Dept. K470-7
  St. Paul, MN 55164–0383, U.S.A.

POSTAGE & HANDLING

(For the U.S., Canada, and Mexico)

- $4 for orders $15 and under
- $5 for orders over $15
- No charge for orders over $100

We ship UPS in the continental United States. We ship standard mail to P.O. boxes. Orders shipped to Alaska, Hawaii, The Virgin Islands, and Puerto Rico are sent first-class mail. Orders shipped to Canada and Mexico are sent surface mail.

International orders: Airmail—add freight equal to price of each book to the total price of order, plus $5.00 for each non-book item (audio tapes, etc.).

Surface mail—Add $1.00 per item.

Allow 4–6 weeks for delivery on all orders.
Postage and handling rates subject to change.

DISCOUNTS

We offer a 20% discount to group leaders or agents. You must order a minimum of 5 copies of the same book to get our special quantity price.

FREE CATALOG

Get a free copy of our color catalog, *New Worlds of Mind and Spirit*. Subscribe for just $10.00 in the United States and Canada ($30.00 overseas, airmail). Many bookstores carry *New Worlds*—ask for it!

Visit our website at www.llewellyn.com for more information.

Mother Nature's Herbal

Judith Griffin, Ph.D.

A Zuni American Indian swallows the juice of goldenrod flowers to ease his sore throat ... an East Indian housewife uses the hot spices of curry to destroy parasites ... an early American settler rubs fresh strawberry juice on her teeth to remove tartar. People throughout the centuries have enjoyed a special relationship with Nature and her many gifts. Now, with *Mother Nature's Herbal,* you can discover how to use a planet full of medicinal and culinary herbs through more than 200 recipes and tonics. Explore the cuisine, beauty secrets and folk remedies of China, the Mediterranean, South America, India, Africa, and North America. The book will also teach you the specific uses of flower essences, chakra balancing, aromatherapy, essential oils, companion planting, organic gardening and theme garden designs.

1-56718-340-9, 448 pp., 7 x 10, 16-pg. color insert, softcover $19.95

To order, call 1–800 THE MOON

Prices subject to change without notice

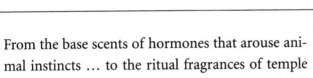

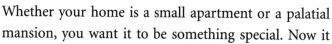

The Magical Household

**Empower Your Home with Love,
Protection, Health and Happiness**

Scott Cunningham and David Harrington

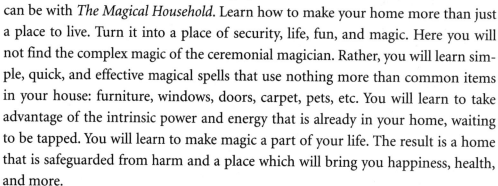

Whether your home is a small apartment or a palatial mansion, you want it to be something special. Now it can be with *The Magical Household*. Learn how to make your home more than just a place to live. Turn it into a place of security, life, fun, and magic. Here you will not find the complex magic of the ceremonial magician. Rather, you will learn simple, quick, and effective magical spells that use nothing more than common items in your house: furniture, windows, doors, carpet, pets, etc. You will learn to take advantage of the intrinsic power and energy that is already in your home, waiting to be tapped. You will learn to make magic a part of your life. The result is a home that is safeguarded from harm and a place which will bring you happiness, health, and more.

0-87542-124-5, 208 pp., 5¼ x 8, illus., softcover   **$9.95**